Bootstrap for ASP.NET MVC

Second Edition

Combine the power of ASP.NET Core with Bootstrap 4 to build elegant, responsive web apps

Pieter van der Westhuizen

BIRMINGHAM - MUMBAI

Bootstrap for ASP.NET MVC

Second Edition

First published: August 2014

Second edition: September 2016

Production reference: 1270916

Published by Packt Publishing Ltd.
Livery Place
35 Livery Street
Birmingham
B3 2PB, UK.
ISBN 978-1-78588-947-9

www.packtpub.com

Credits

Author

Pieter van der Westhuizen

Reviewer

Dony Perdana

Acquisition Editor

Reshma Raman

Content Development Editor

Samantha Gonsalves

Technical Editor

Jayesh Sonawane

Production Coordinator

Arvindkumar Gupta

Copy Editor

Safis Editing

Project Coordinator

Devanshi Doshi

Proofreader

Safis Editing

Indexer

Tejal Soni

Graphics

Jason Monteiro

About the Author

Pieter van der Westhuizen is a freelance software and web developer specializing in ASP.NET MVC, web technologies, and MS Office development. He started his career in web development using classic ASP, Visual InterDev, HoTMetaL, and FrontPage. Pieter has over 16 years of experience in the IT industry and is also one of the people fortunate enough to have his hobby become his full-time profession.

He is also a technology evangelist for Add-in Express (`www.add-in-express.com`), which focuses on tools for Microsoft Office integration.

This is Pieter's second book and he has been blogging since 2007 on his personal blog at `www.mythicalmanmoth.com` and on the Add-in Express blog since 2010. He lives with his wife and two dogs in Pretoria, South Africa.

To everyone who contributed to this book, thank you! A big thanks to the team at Packt Publishing, for their guidance, advice, and professionalism. Thanks to my technical reviewer, Dony Perdana, for patiently reading each chapter, reviewing each line of code, and contributing suggestions. You helped shape this book into what it is. I'd like to express my greatest love and gratitude towards my wife, Andrea, for all her support, impromptu editing sessions, being a soundboard for brainstorming sessions, and the general motivational pep talks during the writing of this book. Lastly, thanks to you for buying this book. I hope this can help you become a better programmer. If you have any questions regarding this book, please visit `www.bootstrapforaspnetmvc.com`.

About the Reviewer

Dony Perdana is an enthusiast and full-stack .NET developer from Indonesia. He has been involved with various banking project solutions for the past 5 years, especially on .NET server side web technologies such as ASP Web API, ASP MVC, ASP Core 1.0, and ServiceStack. He is also proficient with frontend web development, including various JavaScript frameworks (JQuery, AngularJS, BackboneJS, KnockoutJS, and ReactJS).

He developed many applications, including content management systems, real-time and scheduler application, social media apps, web service-based applications.

He has strongly believes that design-pattern practices and agile development can tackle any problem and increase team productivity in software development.

In his spare time, he participates in many learning resources such as reading books, chess, and going to conferences and meetups to keep up with the latest technologies and methodologies for programming. He also helps people on Stack Overflow and contributes to opensource projects on GitHub repositories.

www.PacktPub.com

eBooks, discount offers, and more

Did you know that Packt offers eBook versions of every book published, with PDF and ePub files available? You can upgrade to the eBook version at www.PacktPub.com and as a print book customer, you are entitled to a discount on the eBook copy. Get in touch with us at customercare@packtpub.com for more details.

At www.PacktPub.com, you can also read a collection of free technical articles, sign up for a range of free newsletters and receive exclusive discounts and offers on Packt books and eBooks.

https://www.packtpub.com/mapt

Get the most in-demand software skills with Mapt. Mapt gives you full access to all Packt books and video courses, as well as industry-leading tools to help you plan your personal development and advance your career.

Why subscribe?

- Fully searchable across every book published by Packt
- Copy and paste, print, and bookmark content
- On demand and accessible via a web browser

Table of Contents

Preface   1

Chapter 1: Getting Started with ASP.NET Core and Bootstrap 4   7

   Files included in the Bootstrap distribution   7
      Bootstrap style sheets   8
      Bootstrap JavaScript files   8
      Bootstrap fonts/icons   8
      Bootstrap source files   8
   CSS pre-processors   9
   Creating an empty ASP.NET MVC site and adding Bootstrap manually   9
      Enabling MVC and static files   11
      Creating the default route controller and view   12
   Adding the Bootstrap 4 files using Bower   15
   Compiling the Bootstrap Sass files using Gulp   17
      Adding Gulp npm packages   18
         Enabling Gulp-Sass compilation   20
         Running Gulp tasks   21
         Binding Gulp tasks to Visual Studio events   22
   Installing Font Awesome   23
   Creating a MVC Layout page   25
      Content Delivery Networks   26
   Summary   27

Chapter 2: Using Bootstrap CSS and HTML Elements   29

   The Bootstrap grid system   29
      Bootstrap Grid components   30
         Containers   30
         Rows   30
         Columns   31
   Bootstrap HTML elements   32
      Bootstrap tables   33
         Enabling MVC Scaffolding   33
         Scaffolding an MVC List View page   34
         Styling Bootstrap tables   38
         Bootstrap contextual table classes   41
         Responsive and smaller tables   43
      Bootstrap buttons   44
         Outline buttons   45

Form layout and elements	46
Vertical/basic forms	46
Inline forms	47
Grid-based forms	48
Bootstrap images	49
Bootstrap figures	51
Summary	52
Chapter 3: Using Bootstrap Components	53
The Bootstrap navigation bar	53
Basic navbar	53
Responsive navbar	54
Navbar with dropdown menus	56
Navbar color schemes	57
List groups	58
Badges	60
Media object	61
Breadcrumbs	63
Pagination	64
Input groups	69
Button dropdowns	71
Alerts	72
Progress bars	73
Basic progress bar	74
Contextual progress bars	74
Striped and animated progress bars	75
Cards	75
Summary	77
Chapter 4: Using Bootstrap JavaScript Components	79
Data attributes versus the programmatic API	79
Cascading dropdowns	80
Modal dialogs	84
Modal size and animation	86
Tabs	87
Tooltips	89
Popovers	90
The accordion/collapse component	92
The carousel component	94
Summary	97

Chapter 5: Creating MVC Bootstrap Helper and Tag Helpers   99

  Built-in HTML Helpers   100
  Built-in Tag Helpers   100
  The difference between HTML Helpers and Tag Helpers   101
  Creating HTML Helpers using static methods   102
    Using the static method helper in a view   104
  Creating helpers using extension methods   105
    Using the extension method helper in a view   105
  Creating self-closing helpers   106
    Using the self-closing helper in a view   108
  Creating a Bootstrap button Tag Helper   109
    Using the Bootstrap button Tag Helper   110
  Creating a Bootstrap Alert Tag Helper   111
    Using the Bootstrap Alert Tag Helper   112
  Summary   112

Chapter 6: Converting a Bootstrap HTML Template into a Usable ASP.NET MVC Project   113

  Working with prebuilt HTML templates   113
  Creating the ASP.NET MVC project   116
  Creating the master layout   119
  Adding a view for the home controller   121
  Adding different page views   123
  Adding charts to views   126
    Adding Google Charts to views   126
    Server-side data processing with Google Charts   128
  Summary   131

Chapter 7: Using the jQuery DataTables Plugin with Bootstrap 4   133

  jQuery DataTables   133
  Adding DataTables to your ASP.NET MVC project   134
    Using the DataTables Bower package   134
    Using the CDN   135
    Adding Bootstrap styling to DataTables   135
  Loading and displaying data in jQuery DataTables   136
  DataTables plugins   141
    Date sorting   142
    Rendering   143
  DataTables extensions   143
    The ColReorder extension   144

The ColVis buttons extension 146
The copy and print buttons extension 147
Summary 150
Chapter 8: Creating Bootstrap 4 ASP.NET MVC Sites Using Visual Studio Code 151
What is Visual Studio Code? 152
Installing Visual Studio Code 152
Creating an empty ASP.NET project 154
Scaffolding a project using Yeoman 154
Enabling ASP.NET MVC and static files 156
Adding a default route controller and view 158
Using Bower to add the Bootstrap 4 files 160
Using Gulp to compile the Bootstrap Sass files 162
Creating a MVC layout page 165
Testing the site 166
Summary 166
Appendix: Bootstrap Resources 167
Themes 167
Add-ons 168
Editors and generators 169
Index 171

Preface

Twitter Bootstrap, known simply as Bootstrap, is the leading open source CSS/HTML and JavaScript framework on the Internet. Shortly after its launch, it was the most popular project on GitHub. It is so popular that Microsoft announced at their Build 2013 conference that all the web app project templates in Visual Studio 2013 will use Twitter Bootstrap by default.

One of the main reasons Bootstrap is so prevalent is that it allows developers, many of whom are notoriously bad at user interface design, to build aesthetically pleasing sites with a relatively small amount of effort. Bootstrap also offers a rich ecosystem of free and commercial templates, third-party components, tools, and an active and helpful community.

Using CSS Frameworks and Bootstrap in particular with ASP.NET MVC is a natural fit. Bootstrap takes care of the typography, form layouts, and user interface components, which allows the developer to focus on what they are good at – writing code. This aspect is particularly valuable for smaller development companies who do not necessarily have an in-house designer.

.NET Core is a new and exciting framework written from the ground up. It can be used to develop a variety of applications, not just web applications. It promises the ability to target different platform, such as Linux and Mac as well as smaller deployment footprints. ASP.NET Core has been built upon the .NET Core and is a rewrite of the ASP.NET platform .NET developers have known for many years.

What this book covers

Bootstrap for ASP.NET MVC walks you through the process of creating a fully functioning ASP.NET MVC website, using Bootstrap for its layout and user interface.

Chapter 1, *Getting Started with ASP.NET Core and Bootstrap 4*, introduces you to the files in the Bootstrap 4 distribution, creating an empty ASP.NET site as well as providing an introduction to using Bower and Gulp.

Chapter 2, *Using Bootstrap CSS and HTML Elements*, examines all the various Bootstrap CSS and HTML elements, how to include them in your ASP.NET MVC project, and how to configure and use their various options.

Chapter 3, *Using Bootstrap Components*, makes you familiar with the Bootstrap navigation bar, button groups, alerts, and introduces you to cards.

Chapter 4, *Using Bootstrap JavaScript Components*, guides you through creating cascading dropdowns, modal dialogs and accordions.

Chapter 5, *Creating MVC Bootstrap Helper and Tag Helpers*, teaches you to create a Bootstrap MVC helper as well as a Tag Helper introduced with ASP.NET Core.

Chapter 6, *Converting a Bootstrap HTML Template into a Usable ASP.NET MVC Project*, converts an open source HTML template and makes it ready to be used with ASP.NET MVC.

Chapter 7, *Using the jQuery DataTables Plugin with Bootstrap 4*, demonstrates how to use the powerful jQuery DataTables plugin with Bootstrap and ASP.NET in order to show tabular data.

Chapter 8, *Creating Bootstrap 4 ASP.NET MVC Sites Using Visual Studio Code*, shows you how to use the free Visual Studio Code editor to create ASP.NET projects.

Appendix, *Bootstrap Resources*, gives you a list of Bootstrap resources available on the Internet.

What you need for this book

To get the most out of this book, you'll need Visual Studio 2015 and a modern browser. All examples have been tested with Visual Studio 2015, Google Chrome, and Mozilla Firefox. The book would be beneficial to those with entry-level up to advanced-level experience of ASP.NET MVC development, as well as limited experience in Bootstrap.

Who this book is for

This book is for ASP.NET MVC developers who would like to know how to incorporate Bootstrap into their projects. ASP.NET MVC developers could also benefit from the chapters covering advanced topics, such as creating helpers and using the jQuery Data-tables plugin. If you have limited experience with ASP.NET MVC and Bootstrap, this book can serve as a primer to these technologies.

Conventions

In this book, you will find a number of text styles that distinguish between different kinds of information. Here are some examples of these styles and an explanation of their meaning.

Code words in text, database table names, folder names, filenames, file extensions, pathnames, dummy URLs, user input, and Twitter handles are shown as follows: "Double-click on the `project.json` file inside the Solution Explorer in Visual Studio"

A block of code is set as follows:

```
public void ConfigureServices(IServiceCollection services)
    {
        services.AddMvc();
    }
```

Any command-line input or output is written as follows:

```
npm install -g yo grunt-cli generator-aspnet bower
```

New terms and **important words** are shown in bold. Words that you see on the screen, for example, in menus or dialog boxes, appear in the text like this: "Select the **Empty** project template from the **New ASP.NET Core Web Application (.NET Core)** Project dialog window and click on **OK**"

Warnings or important notes appear in a box like this.

Tips and tricks appear like this.

Reader feedback

Feedback from our readers is always welcome. Let us know what you think about this book-what you liked or disliked. Reader feedback is important for us as it helps us develop titles that you will really get the most out of. To send us general feedback, simply e-mail feedback@packtpub.com, and mention the book's title in the subject of your message. If there is a topic that you have expertise in and you are interested in either writing or contributing to a book, see our author guide at www.packtpub.com/authors.

Customer support

Now that you are the proud owner of a Packt book, we have a number of things to help you to get the most from your purchase.

Downloading the example code

You can download the example code files for this book from https://github.com/Pieterv dw/bootstrap-for-aspnetmvc or from your account at http://www.packtpub.com. If you purchased this book elsewhere, you can visit http://www.packtpub.com/support and register to have the files e-mailed directly to you.

You can download the code files by following these steps:

1. Log in or register to our website using your e-mail address and password.
2. Hover the mouse pointer on the **SUPPORT** tab at the top.
3. Click on **Code Downloads & Errata**.
4. Enter the name of the book in the **Search** box.
5. Select the book for which you're looking to download the code files.
6. Choose from the drop-down menu where you purchased this book from.
7. Click on **Code Download**.

Once the file is downloaded, please make sure that you unzip or extract the folder using the latest version of:

- WinRAR / 7-Zip for Windows
- Zipeg / iZip / UnRarX for Mac
- 7-Zip / PeaZip for Linux

We also have other code bundles from our rich catalog of books and videos available at `https://github.com/PacktPublishing/`. Check them out!

Downloading the color images of this book

We also provide you with a PDF file that has color images of the screenshots/diagrams used in this book. The color images will help you better understand the changes in the output. You can download this file from `http://www.packtpub.com/sites/default/files/downloads/BootstrapforASPNETMVC_ColorImages.pdf`.

Errata

Although we have taken every care to ensure the accuracy of our content, mistakes do happen. If you find a mistake in one of our books-maybe a mistake in the text or the code- we would be grateful if you could report this to us. By doing so, you can save other readers from frustration and help us improve subsequent versions of this book. If you find any errata, please report them by visiting `http://www.packtpub.com/submit-errata`, selecting your book, clicking on the **Errata Submission Form** link, and entering the details of your errata. Once your errata are verified, your submission will be accepted and the errata will be uploaded to our website or added to any list of existing errata under the Errata section of that title.

To view the previously submitted errata, go to `https://www.packtpub.com/books/content/support` and enter the name of the book in the search field. The required information will appear under the **Errata** section.

Piracy

Piracy of copyrighted material on the Internet is an ongoing problem across all media. At Packt, we take the protection of our copyright and licenses very seriously. If you come across any illegal copies of our works in any form on the Internet, please provide us with the location address or website name immediately so that we can pursue a remedy.

Please contact us at `copyright@packtpub.com` with a link to the suspected pirated material.

We appreciate your help in protecting our authors and our ability to bring you valuable content.

Questions

If you have a problem with any aspect of this book, you can contact us
at questions@packtpub.com, and we will do our best to address the problem.

1
Getting Started with ASP.NET Core and Bootstrap 4

As developers, we can find it difficult to create great-looking user interfaces from scratch when using HTML and CSS. This is especially hard when developers have extensive experience developing Windows Forms applications. Microsoft introduced Web Forms to remove the complexities of building websites and to ease the switch from Windows Forms to the Web. This in turn makes it very hard for Web Forms developers, and even harder for Windows Forms developers, to switch to ASP.NET MVC. Bootstrap is a set of stylized components, plugins, and a layout grid that takes care of the heavy lifting. Microsoft has included Bootstrap in all ASP.NET MVC project templates since 2013.

In this chapter, we will cover the following topics:

- Files included in the Bootstrap distribution
- How to create an empty ASP.NET site and enable MVC and static files
- Adding the Bootstrap files using Bower
- Automatically compile the Bootstrap Sass files using Gulp
- Installing additional icon sets
- How to create a Layout file that references the Bootstrap files

Files included in the Bootstrap distribution

In order to get acquainted with the files inside the Bootstrap distribution, you need to download its source files. At the time of writing, Bootstrap 4 was still in Alpha, and its source files can be downloaded from `http://v4-alpha.getbootstrap.com`.

Bootstrap style sheets

Do not be alarmed by the amount of files inside the `css` folder. This folder contains four `.css` files and two `.map` files. We only need to include the `bootstrap.css` file in our project for the Bootstrap styles to be applied to our pages. The `bootstrap.min.css` file is simply a minified version of the aforementioned file. The `.map` files can be ignored for the project we'll be creating. These files are used as a type of debug symbol (similar to the `.pdb` files in Visual Studio), which allows developers to live edit their preprocessor source files, something that is beyond the scope of this book.

Bootstrap JavaScript files

The `js` folder contains two files. All the Bootstrap plugins are contained in the `bootstrap.js` file. The `bootstrap.min.js` file is simply a minified version of the aforementioned file. Before including the file in your project, make sure that you have a reference to the jQuery library because all Bootstrap plugins require jQuery.

Bootstrap fonts/icons

Bootstrap 3 uses Glyphicons to display various icons and glyphs in Bootstrap sites. Bootstrap 4 will no longer ship with glyphicons included, but you still have the option to include it manually or to include your own icons. The following two icon sets are good alternatives to Glyphicons:

- Font Awesome, available from `http://fontawesome.io/`
- GitHub's Octicons, available from `https://octicons.github.com/`

Bootstrap source files

Before you can get started with Bootstrap, you first need to download the Bootstrap source files. At the time of writing, Bootstrap 4 was at version 4 Alpha 3. You have a few choices when adding Bootstrap to you project. You can download the compiled CSS and JavaScript files or you can use a number of package managers to install the Bootstrap Sass source to your project.

In this chapter, you'll be using Bower to add the Bootstrap 4 source files to your project.

 For a complete list of Bootstrap 4 Alpha installation sources, visit `http://v4-alpha.getbootstrap.com/getting-started/download/`.

CSS pre-processors

CSS pre-processors process code written in a pre-processed language, such as LESS or Sass, and convert it into standard CSS, which in turn can be interpreted by any standard web browser. CSS pre-processors extend CSS by adding features that allow variables, mixins, and functions.

The benefits of using CSS pre-processors are that they are not bound by any limitations of CSS. CSS pre-processors can give you more functionality and control over your style sheets and allow you to write more maintainable, flexible, and extendable CSS.

CSS pre-processors can also help to reduce the amount of CSS and assist with the management of large and complex style sheets that can become harder to maintain as the size and complexity increases.

In essence, CSS pre-processors such as Less and Sass enable programmatic control over your style sheets.

Bootstrap moved their source files from Less to Sass with version 4. Less and Sass are very alike in that they share a similar syntax as well as features such as variables, mixins, partials, and nesting, to name but a few.

Less was influenced by Sass, and later on, Sass was influenced by Less when it adopted CSS-like block formatting, which worked very well for Less.

Creating an empty ASP.NET MVC site and adding Bootstrap manually

The default ASP.NET 5 project template in Visual Studio 2015 Update 3 currently adds Bootstrap 3 to the project. In order to use Bootstrap 4 in your ASP.NET project, you'll need to create an empty ASP.NET project and add the Bootstrap 4 files manually.

To create a project that uses Bootstrap 4, complete the following process:

1. In Visual Studio 2015, select **New | Project** from the **File** menu or use the keyboard shortcut *Ctrl + Shift + N*.
2. From the New Project dialog window, select **ASP.NET Core Web Application (.NET Core)**, which you'll find under **Templates | Visual C# | Web**.

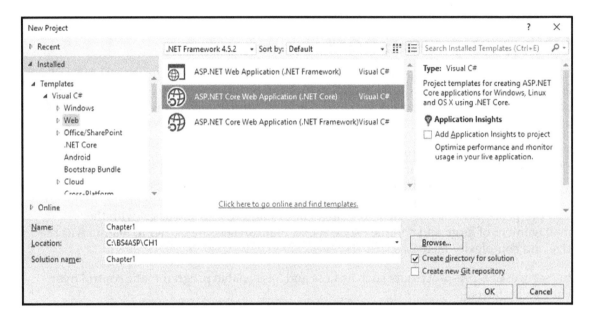

3. Select the **Empty** project template from the **New ASP.NET Core Web Application (.NET Core)** Project dialog window and click on **OK**.

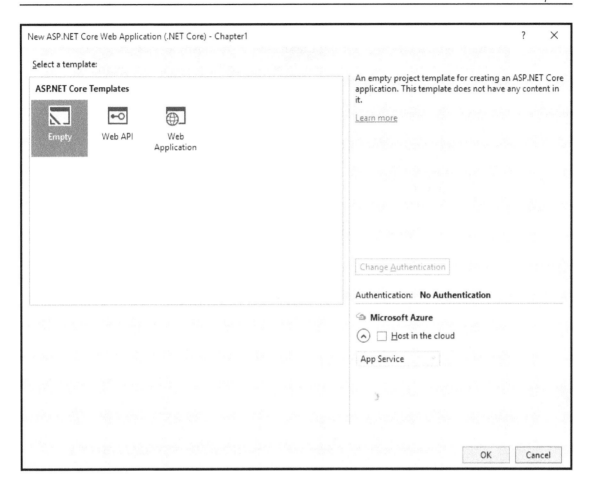

Enabling MVC and static files

The previous steps will create a blank ASP.NET Core project. Running the project as-is will only show a simple Hello World output in your browser. In order for it to serve static files and enable MVC, we'll need to complete the following steps:

1. Double-click on the `project.json` file inside the Solution Explorer in Visual Studio.
2. Add the following two lines to the *dependencies* section, and save the `project.json` file:

   ```
   "Microsoft.AspNetCore.Mvc": "1.0.0",
   "Microsoft.AspNetCore.StaticFiles": "1.0.0"
   ```

3. You should see a yellow colored notification inside the Visual Studio Solution Explorer with a message stating that it is busy restoring packages.
4. Open the `Startup.cs` file. To enable MVC for the project, change the `ConfigureServices` method to the following:

```
public void ConfigureServices(IServiceCollection services)
{
    services.AddMvc();
}
```

5. Finally, update the `Configure` method to the following code:

```
public void Configure(IApplicationBuilder app, IHostingEnvironment
env, ILoggerFactory loggerFactory)
{
    loggerFactory.AddConsole();

    if (env.IsDevelopment())
    {
        app.UseDeveloperExceptionPage();
    }

    app.UseStaticFiles();

    app.UseMvc(routes =>
    {
        routes.MapRoute(
        name: "default",
        template: "{controller=Home}/{action=Index}/{id?}");
    });
}
```

6. The preceding code will enable logging and the serving of static files such as images, style sheets, and JavaScript files. It will also set the default MVC route.

Creating the default route controller and view

When creating an empty ASP.NET Core project, no default controller or views will be created by default. In the previous steps, we've created a default route to the Index action of the Home controller. In order for this to work, we first need to complete the following steps:

1. In the Visual Studio Solution Explorer, right-click on the project name and select **Add** | **New Folder** from the context menu.

2. Name the new folder `Controllers`.

3. Add another folder called `Views`.

4. Right-click on the `Controllers` folder and select **Add | New Item...** from the context menu.

5. Select **MVC Controller Class** from the **Add New Item** dialog, located under **.NET Core | ASP.NET**, and click on **Add**. The default name when adding a new controller will be `HomeController.cs`:

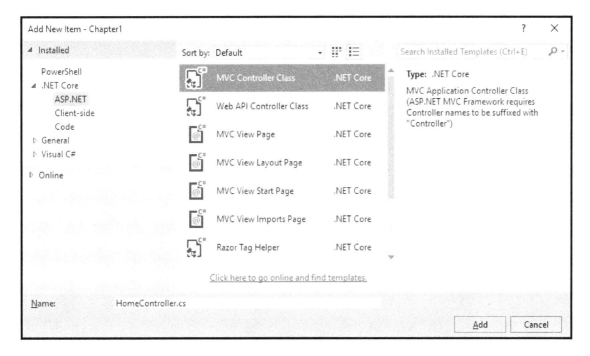

6. Next, we'll need to add a subfolder for the `HomeController` in the `Views` folder. Right-click on the `Views` folder and select **Add | New Folder** from the context menu.

7. Name the new folder `Home`.

8. Right-click on the newly created `Home` folder and select **Add | New Item...** from the context menu.

9. Select the **MVC View Page** item, located under **.NET Core | ASP.NET**; from the list, make sure the filename is `Index.cshtml` and click on the **Add** button:

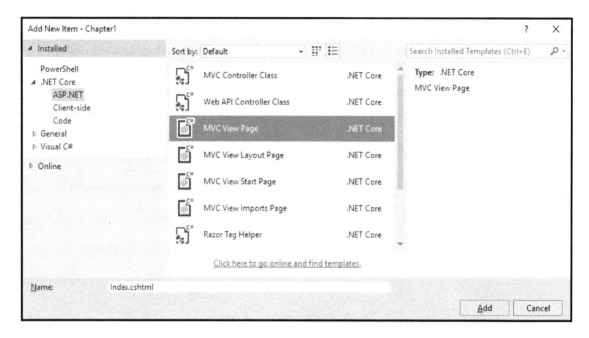

10. Your project layout should resemble the following in the Visual Studio Solution Explorer:

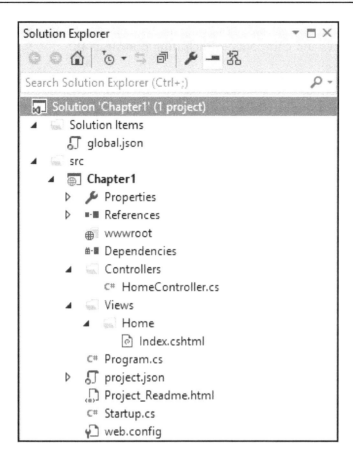

Adding the Bootstrap 4 files using Bower

With ASP.NET 5 and Visual Studio 2015, Microsoft provided the ability to use Bower as a client-side package manager. Bower is a package manager for web frameworks and libraries that is already very popular in the web development community.

 You can read more about Bower and search the packages it provides by visiting `http://bower.io/`.

Microsoft's decision to allow the use of Bower and package managers other than NuGet for client-side dependencies is because it already has such a rich ecosystem.

Do not fear! NuGet is not going away. You can still use NuGet to install libraries and components, including Bootstrap 4!

To add the Bootstrap 4 source files to your project, you need to follow these steps:

1. Right-click on the project name inside Visual Studio's Solution Explorer and select **Add** | **New Item...**.
2. Under **.NET Core** | **Client-side**, select the **Bower Configuration File** item, make sure the filename is bower.json and click on **Add**, as shown here:

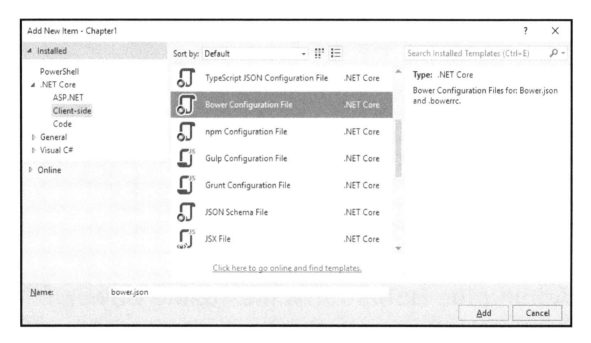

3. If not already open, double-click on the bower.json file to open it and add Bootstrap 4 to the dependencies array. The code for the file should look similar to the following:

```
{
    "name": "asp.net",
    "private": true,
    "dependencies": {
    "bootstrap": "v4.0.0-alpha.3"
    }
}
```

4. Save the `bower.json` file.

5. Once you've saved the `bower.json` file, Visual Studio will automatically download the dependencies into the `wwwroot/lib` folder of your project. In the case of Bootstrap 4 it also depends on **jQuery and Tether**. You'll notice that jQuery and Tether has also been downloaded as part of the Bootstrap dependency.

6. After you've added Bootstrap to your project, your project layout should look similar to the following screenshot:

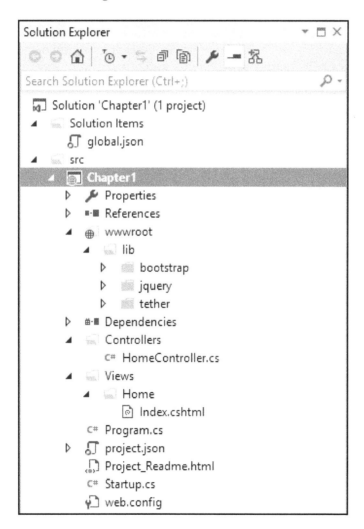

Compiling the Bootstrap Sass files using Gulp

When adding Bootstrap 4, you'll notice that the `bootstrap` folder contains a subfolder called `dist`. Inside the `dist` folder, there are ready-to-use Bootstrap CSS and JavaScript files that you can use as-is if you do not want to change any of the default Bootstrap colours or properties.

However, because the source Sass files were also added, this gives you extra flexibility in customizing the look and feel of your web application. For instance, the default colour of the base Bootstrap distribution is gray; if you want to change all the default colours to shades of blue, it would be tedious work to find and replace all references to the colours in the CSS file.

For example, if you open the `_variables.scss` file, located in `wwwroot/lib/bootstrap/scss`, you'll notice the following code:

```
$gray-dark:            #373a3c !default;
$gray:                 #55595c !default;
$gray-light:           #818a91 !default;
$gray-lighter:         #eceeef !default;
$gray-lightest:        #f7f7f9 !default;
```

We're not going to go into too much detail regarding Sass in this book, but the `$` in front of the names in the code above indicates that these are variables used to compile the final CSS file. In essence, changing the values of these variables will change the colors to the new values we've specified, when the Sass file is compiled.

 To learn more about Sass, head over to `http://sass-lang.com/`.

Adding Gulp npm packages

We'll need to add the `gulp` and `gulp-sass` Node packages to our solution in order to be able to perform actions using Gulp. To accomplish this, you will need to use **npm**.

npm is the default package manager for the Node.js runtime environment.
You can read more about it at `https://www.npmjs.com/`.

To add the `gulp` and `gulp-sass npm` packages to your `ASP.NET` project, complete the
following steps:

1. Right-click on your project name inside the Visual Studio Solution Explorer and
   select **Add | New Item...** from the project context menu.
2. Find the **npm Configuration File** item, located under **.NET Core | Client-side**.
   Keep its name as `package.json` and click on **Add**.

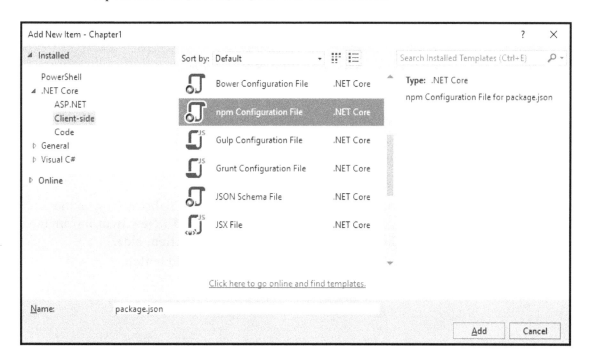

3. If not already open, double-click on the newly added `package.json` file and add
   the following two dependencies to the `devDependencies` array inside the file:

```
"devDependencies": {
  "gulp": "3.9.1",
  "gulp-sass": "2.3.2"
}
```

This will add version 3.9.1 of the gulp package and version 2.3.2 of the gulp-sass package to your project. At the time of writing, these were the latest versions. Your version numbers might differ.

Enabling Gulp-Sass compilation

Visual Studio does not compile Sass files to CSS by default without installing extensions, but we can enable it using Gulp.

Gulp is a JavaScript toolkit used to stream client-side code through a series of processes when an event is triggered during build. Gulp can be used to automate and simplify development and repetitive tasks, such as the following:

- Minify CSS
- JavaScript and image files, Rename files
- Combine CSS files

Learn more about Gulp at http://gulpjs.com/.

Before you can use Gulp to compile your Sass files to CSS, you need to complete the following tasks:

1. Add a new **Gulp Configuration File** to your project by right-clicking on the project name in the Solution Explorer and selecting **Add | New Item...** from the context menu. The location of the item is **.NET Core | Client-side**.
2. Keep the filename as gulpfile.js and click on the **Add** button.

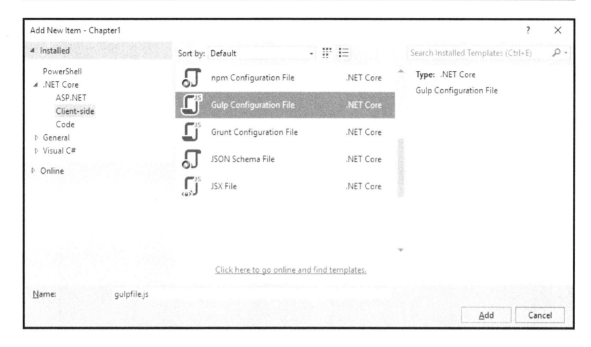

3. Change the code inside the `gulpfile.js` file to the following:

```
var gulp = require('gulp');
var gulpSass = require('gulp-sass');
gulp.task('compile-sass', function () {
  gulp.src('./wwwroot/lib/bootstrap/scss/bootstrap.scss')
  .pipe(gulpSass()) .pipe(gulp.dest('./wwwroot/css'));
  });
```

The code in the preceding step first declares that we require the gulp and gulp-sass packages, and then creates a new task called **compile-sass** that will compile the Sass source file located at `/wwwroot/lib/bootstrap/scss/bootstrap.scss` and output the result to the `/wwwroot/css` folder.

Running Gulp tasks

With the `gulpfile.js` properly configured, you are now ready to run your first Gulp task to compile the Bootstrap Sass to CSS. Accomplish this by completing the following steps:

Right-click on `gulpfile.js` in the Visual Studio Solution Explorer and choose **Task Runner Explorer** from the context menu.

You should see all tasks declared in the `gulpfile.js` listed underneath the **Tasks** node. If you do not see tasks listed, click on the **Refresh** button, located on the left-hand side of the **Task Runner Explorer** window.

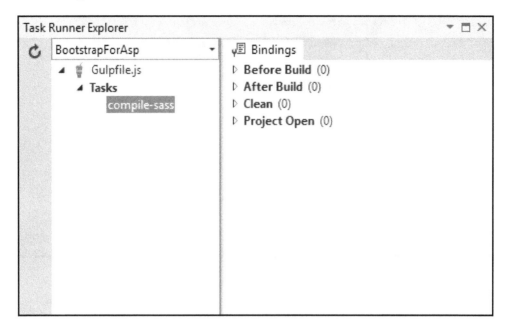

To run the compile-sass task, right-click on it and select **Run** from the context menu.

Gulp will compile the Bootstrap 4 Sass files and output the CSS to the specified folder.

Binding Gulp tasks to Visual Studio events

Right-clicking on every task in the **Task Runner Explorer,** in order to execute each, could involve a lot of manual steps. Luckily, Visual Studio allows us to bind tasks to the following events inside Visual Studio:

- Before Build
- After Build
- Clean
- Project Open

If, for example, we would like to compile the Bootstrap 4 Sass files before building our project, simply select **Before Build** from the **Bindings** context menu of the Visual Studio **Task Runner Explorer**:

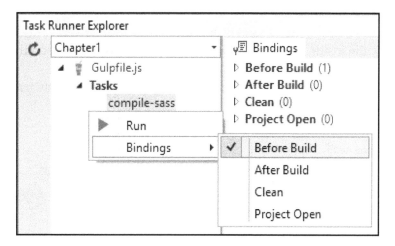

Visual Studio will add the following line of code to the top of gulpfile.js to tell the compiler to run the task before building the project:

```
/// <binding BeforeBuild='compile-sass' />
```

Installing Font Awesome

Bootstrap 4 no longer comes bundled with the Glyphicons icon set. However, there are a number of free alternatives available for use with your Bootstrap and other projects. Font Awesome is a very good alternative to Glyphicons that provides you with 650 icons to use and is free for commercial use.

Learn more about Font Awesome by visiting https://fortawesome.gith ub.io/Font-Awesome/.

You can add a reference to **Font Awesome** manually, but since we already have everything set up in our project, the quickest option is to simply install Font Awesome using Bower and compile it to the Bootstrap style sheet using Gulp. To accomplish this, follow these steps:

1. Open the `bower.json` file, which is located in your project route. If you do not see the file inside the **Visual Studio Solution Explorer**, click on the **Show All Files** button on the **Solution Explorer** toolbar.

2. Add `font-awesome` as a dependency to the file. The complete listing of the `bower.json` file is as follows:

```
{
  "name": "asp.net",
  "private": true,
  "dependencies": {
  "bootstrap": "v4.0.0-alpha.3",
  "font-awesome": "4.6.3"
  }
}
```

3. Visual Studio will download the Font Awesome source files and add a `font-awesome` subfolder to the `wwwroot/lib/` folder inside your project.

4. Copy the `fonts` folder located under `wwwroot/font-awesome` to the `wwwroot` folder.

5. Next, open the `bootstrap.scss` file located in the `wwwroot/lib/bootstrap/scss` folder and add the following line at the end of the file:

```
$fa-font-path: "/fonts";
@import "../../font-awesome/scss/font-awesome.scss";
```

6. Run the compile-sass task via the **Task Runner Explorer** to recompile the Bootstrap Sass.

The preceding steps will include Font Awesome in your Bootstrap CSS file, which in turn will enable you to use it inside your project by including the mark-up demonstrated here:

```
<i class="fa fa-pied-piper-alt"></i>
```

Creating a MVC Layout page

The final step for using Bootstrap 4 in your ASP.NET MVC project is to create a Layout page that will contain all the necessary CSS and JavaScript files in order to include Bootstrap components in your pages. To create a Layout page, follow these steps:

1. Add a new sub folder called `Shared` to the `Views` folder.
2. Add a new **MVC View Layout Page** to the `Shared` folder. The item can be found in the **.NET Core | Server-side** category of the **Add New Item** dialog.
3. Name the file `_Layout.cshtml` and click on the **Add** button:

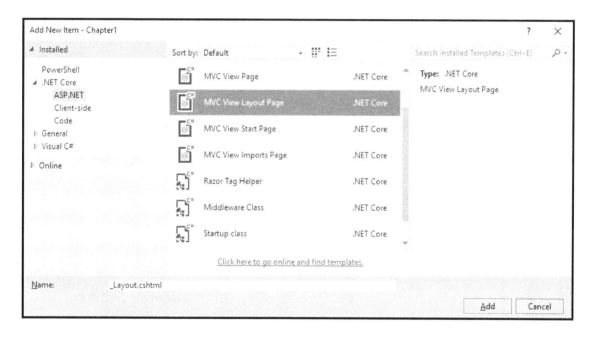

4. With the current project layout, add the following HTML to the `_Layout.cshtml` file:

```
<!DOCTYPE html>
<html lang="en">
  <head>
    <meta charset="utf-8">
    <meta name="viewport" content="width=device-width,
     initial-scale=1, shrink-to-fit=no">
    <meta http-equiv="x-ua-compatible" content="ie=edge">
    <title>@ViewBag.Title</title>
    <link rel="stylesheet" href="~/css/bootstrap.css" />
```

```
    </head>
    <body>
      @RenderBody()

        <script src="~/lib/jquery/dist/jquery.js"></script>
        <script src="~/lib/bootstrap/dist/js/bootstrap.js"></script>
    </body>
    </html>
```

5. Finally, add a new **MVC View Start Page** to the `Views` folder called `_ViewStart.cshtml`. The `_ViewStart.cshtml` file is used to specify common code shared by all views.

6. Add the following Razor markup to the `_ViewStart.cshtml` file:

```
@{
    Layout = "_Layout";
}
```

7. In the preceding mark-up, a reference to the Bootstrap CSS file that was generated using the Sass source files and Gulp is added to the `<head>` element of the file. In the `<body>` tag, the `@RenderBody` method is invoked using **Razor** syntax.

8. Finally, at the bottom of the file, just before the closing `</body>` tag, a reference to the jQuery library and the Bootstrap JavaScript file is added. Note that jQuery must always be referenced before the Bootstrap JavaScript file.

Content Delivery Networks

You could also reference the jQuery and Bootstrap library from a **Content Delivery Network (CDN)**. This is a good approach to use when adding references to the most widely used JavaScript libraries. This should allow your site to load faster if the user has already visited a site that uses the same library from the same CDN, because the library will be cached in their browser.

In order to reference the Bootstrap and jQuery libraries from a CDN, change the `<script>` tags to the following:

```
<script src="https://code.jquery.com/jquery-3.1.0.js"></script>
<script
src="https://maxcdn.bootstrapcdn.com/bootstrap/4.0.0-alpha.2/js/bootstrap.m
in.js"></script>
```

 You can download the example code files for this book from `https://git hub.com/Pietervdw/bootstrap-for-aspnetmvc`.

There are a number of CDNs available on the Internet; listed here are some of the more popular options:

- MaxCDN: `https://www.maxcdn.com/`
- Google Hosted Libraries: `https://developers.google.com/speed/libraries/`
- CloudFlare: `https://www.cloudflare.com/`
- Amazon CloudFront: `https://aws.amazon.com/cloudfront/`

Summary

In this chapter, you learned how to create an empty ASP.NET project and how to add the Bootstrap 4 source files using Bower. You were also introduced to using Gulp to perform tasks such as compiling Sass file to CSS.

In the next chapter, you'll be introduced to Bootstrap's CSS and HTML elements and learn how to use them in the design and layout of your site.

2
Using Bootstrap CSS and HTML Elements

Bootstrap provides a wide range of HTML elements and CSS classes as well as an advanced grid system to aid in laying out your web page designs. These classes and elements include utilities to assist with typography, code formatting, table, and form layouts, to name a few.

All CSS classes and HTML elements, combined with the mobile-first fluid grid system, enable developers to build intuitive web interfaces quickly and easily without having to worry about the nuts and bolts of enabling responsiveness for smaller device screens and styling user interface elements.

In this chapter, we will cover the following topics:

- The Bootstrap grid system
- Bootstrap tables and buttons
- Laying out different Bootstrap forms
- Enabling ASP.NET MVC scaffolding templates
- Using images in Bootstrap and configuring the images to be responsive

The Bootstrap grid system

In 2015 Google said *"more Google searches take place on mobile devices than on computers in 10 countries including the US and Japan"*. (`http://adwords.blogspot.co.za/215/5/building-for-next-moment.html`) This means that chances are more people are browsing your website with a mobile device than a traditional desktop computer.

The Bootstrap grid system is mobile-first, which means it is designed to target devices with smaller displays and then grow as the display size increases. It uses a 12-column layout with different tiers for each media query range.

Bootstrap Grid components

Think of the Bootstrap grid system as similar to a traditional HTML table. It primarily consists of three components:

- Containers
- Rows
- Columns

Containers

Containers are required in order to use the Bootstrap grid system, and are used to wrap and center the page content and to specify a proper width for the layout. As the name implies, it acts as a container for the grid's rows and columns and is a standard <div> element with the class name `.container`, for fixed width or `.container-fluid` for full width. For example:

```
<div class="container"></div>
```

The fixed width `.container` class name will change the **max-width** of the element at each responsive breakpoint, whereas the `.container-fluid` class name will always set the elements width to 100%.

Rows

Keeping the analogy of a table, with the Bootstrap grid system in mind, rows are similar to rows in a table. Each row can consist of up to 12 columns and only columns are allowed to contain content. A row is a simple <div> element with a class name of `.row` inside a <div> element with a `.container` class name or `.container-fluid`. An example of a simple row inside a container looks as follows:

```
<div class="container">
    <div class="row">
    </div>
</div>
```

Columns

Columns in the Bootstrap Grid are used to divide a row in defined sections, and a row cannot have more than 12 columns. Columns sizes have five tiers, which are used for sizing depending on the device's screen size:

- Extra large
- Large
- Medium
- Small
- Extra small

The five tiers are used to create a responsive breakpoint, which in turn is used to specify the layout for different device sizes. The following table explains the different tiers:

Class name	Type of device	Minimum width
col-xs-*	Phones in portrait	< 34 em
col-sm-*	Phones in landscape	34 em
col-md-*	Tablets	48 em
Col-lg-*	Desktops	62 em
Col-xl-*	High-resolution desktops	75 em

As mentioned earlier, a Bootstrap row can be divided into 12 columns. When laying out your webpage, keep in mind that all columns combined should be a total of 12. To illustrate this, consider the following HTML:

```
<div class="container">
    <div class="row">
    <div class="col-md-3" style="background-color:green;">
        <h3>green</h3>
    </div>
        <div class="col-md-6" style="background-color:red;">
        <h3>red</h3>
    </div>
        <div class="col-md-3" style="background-color:blue;">
        <h3>blue</h3>
    </div>
    </div>
</div>
```

In the preceding code, we have a container `<div>` element with one child row `<div>` element. The row div in turn has three columns. You will notice that two of the columns have a class name of `.col-md-3`and one of the columns has a class name of `.col-md-6`. Combined, they add up to 12.

The preceding code will work well on all medium devices and higher. To preserve the preceding layout on devices with smaller resolutions, you'll need to combine the various CSS grid classes. For example, to allow our layout to work on tablets, phones, medium and large-sized desktop displays, change the HTML to the following:

```
<div class="container">
    <div class="row">
    <div class="col-xs-3 col-sm-3 col-md-3 col-lg-3"
     style="background-color:green;">
            <h3>green</h3>
        </div>
        <div class="col-xs-6 col-sm-6 col-md-6 col-lg-6"
         style="background-color:red;">
            <h3>red</h3>
        </div>
        <div class="col-xs-3 col-sm-3 col-md-3 col-lg-3"
         style="background-color:blue;">
            <h3>blue</h3>
        </div>
    </div>
</div>
```

By adding the `.col-xs-*` and `.col-sm-*` class names to the `div` elements, we'll ensure that our layout will appear the same in a wide range of device resolutions.

Bootstrap HTML elements

Bootstrap provides a host of different HTML elements that are styled and ready to use. These elements include the following:

- Tables
- Buttons
- Forms
- Images

Bootstrap tables

Bootstrap provides default styling for HTML tables with a few options to customize their layouts and behaviors. The default ASP.NET MVC scaffolding automatically adds the `.table` class name to the table element when generating a **List** view.

Enabling MVC Scaffolding

In the previous chapter, we created an empty ASP.NET Core project. In order to enable the built-in Visual Studio Scaffolding and because the new ASP.NET's approach is to only add the dependencies you need, we have to manually add the required dependencies to the project by completing the following tasks:

1. Open the project you created in `Chapter 1`, *Getting Started with ASP.NET Core and Bootstrap 4*, in Visual Studio.
2. Locate the `project.json` file in the project's root folder and double-click it to edit.
3. Add or update the following dependencies to the dependencies array inside the file:

```
"Microsoft.AspNetCore.Mvc": "1.0.0",
"Microsoft.AspNetCore.StaticFiles": "1.0.0",
"Microsoft.AspNetCore.Razor.Tools": {
  "version": "1.0.0-preview2-final",
  "type": "build"
},
"Microsoft.VisualStudio.Web.CodeGeneration.Tools": {
  "version": "1.0.0-preview2-final",
  "type": "build"
},
"Microsoft.VisualStudio.Web.CodeGenerators.Mvc": {
  "version": "1.0.0-preview2-final",
  "type": "build"
}
```

4. Next, add the following to the tools array in the `project.json` file:

```
"Microsoft.VisualStudio.Web.CodeGeneration.Tools": {
  "version": "1.0.0-preview2-final",
  "imports": [
   "portable-net45+win8"
   ]
}
```

5. The added dependencies and tools will enable the MVC-specific scaffolding templates to Visual Studio. If successful, you should see a **New Scaffolded Item...** entry in the **Add** context menu of the Visual Studio Solution Explorer. Here is a screenshot to illustrate the new menu item:

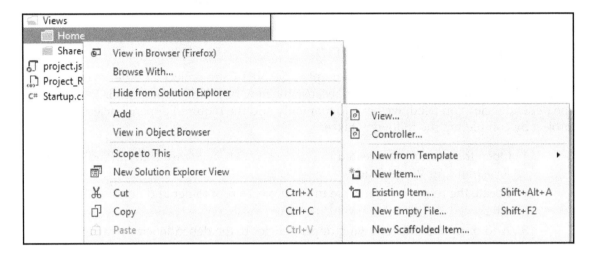

Scaffolding an MVC List View page

To scaffold an MVC View that will automatically include a Bootstrap table, follow these steps:

1. Create a new folder called `Models` in your project.

2. Create a new view model class in the project's `Models` folder called `ProductModel.cs`. This class will contain six properties and its code is as follows:

```
public class ProductModel
{public int Id { get; set; }
public string Name { get; set; }
public decimal UnitPrice { get; set; }
public int UnitsInStock { get; set; }
public bool Discontinued { get; set; }
public string Status { get; set; }
}
```

3. Next, add a new empty`ProductsController` and only add one action result, called `Index`, to it. The controller's filename should be `ProductsController.cs` and it should be created inside the `Controllers` folder. The code for the class is as follows:

```
public class ProductsController : Controller
{
    public IActionResult Index()
  {
        var model = new List<ProductModel>();
        var product1 = new ProductModel { Name = "Chai",
        UnitPrice = 18, UnitsInStock = 35, Discontinued = false,
        Id = 1, Status = "active" };
        var product2 = new ProductModel { Name = "Chang",
        UnitPrice =19, UnitsInStock = 17, Discontinued = false,
        Id = 2, Status = "success" };
        var product3 = new ProductModel { Name = "Aniseed Syrup",
        UnitPrice = 10, UnitsInStock = 13, Discontinued = false,
        Id = 3, Status = "info" };
        var product4 = new ProductModel { Name = "Pavlova",
        UnitPrice =17, UnitsInStock = 29, Discontinued = false,
        Id = 4, Status = "warning" };
        var product5 = new ProductModel { Name = "Carnarvon Tigers",
        UnitPrice = 62, UnitsInStock = 42, Discontinued = true,
        Id = 5, Status = "danger" };
        model.AddRange(new[] { product1, product2, product3, product4,
        product5 });
        return View(model);
    }
}
```

The preceding code initialized a new **List** object, called `model`, containing a collection of the `ProductViewModel` class. Five new `ProductViewModel` objects were created with sample product data and then added to the `model` list. The `model` list was then passed to the view.

Do not be dismayed about the amount of work it takes to enable scaffolding for MVC. These steps are only required when creating an empty ASP.NET project. The default MVC project template will automatically add all the required code configuration and dependencies. However, bear in mind that the default MVC project, at the time of writing, still uses Bootstrap 3.

To scaffold a view that will include a Bootstrap table containing the list of products we've created in the `Index` action, complete the following steps:

1. Create a new subfolder called `Products` in the project's `Views` folder.
2. Right-click on the newly added `Products` folder and select **Add | View...**.
3. In the **Add | View...** dialog windows, set the following field values as shown in the following screenshot:

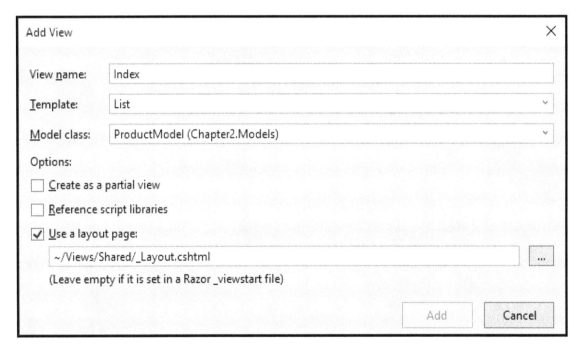

4. Click on the **Add** button, and Visual Studio will scaffold a view containing a Bootstrap table with the column headings containing the names of the properties of the `ProductModel` class.

5. The default ASP.NET MVC scaffolding will generate a basic `<table>` element with a class name of `.table`. We'll change the default-generated markup by adding a **table head element** (`<thead>`), which will be used to define the column headings for the table.

6. This element will be followed by a **table body element** (`<tbody>`). The table body element will contain the actual row data. The resulting markup will look like the following:

```
<table class="table">
    <thead>
        <tr>
          <th>
            @Html.DisplayNameFor(model => model.Discontinued)
          </th>
          <th>
            @Html.DisplayNameFor(model => model.Name)
          </th>
          <th>
            @Html.DisplayNameFor(model => model.Status)
          </th>
          <th>
            @Html.DisplayNameFor(model => model.UnitPrice)
          </th>
          <th>
            @Html.DisplayNameFor(model => model.UnitsInStock)
          </th>
          <th></th>
        </tr>
    </thead>
    <tbody>
        @foreach (var item in Model)
         {
          <tr>
           <td>
            @Html.DisplayFor(modelItem => item.Discontinued)
           </td>
            <td>
              @Html.DisplayFor(modelItem => item.Name)
            </td>
            <td>
              @Html.DisplayFor(modelItem => item.Status)
            </td>
            <td>
              @Html.DisplayFor(modelItem => item.UnitPrice)
            </td>
            <td>
```

```
                    @Html.DisplayFor(modelItem => item.UnitsInStock)
                </td>
                <td>
            <a asp-action="Edit" asp-route-id="@item.Id">Edit</a> |
            <a asp-action="Details" asp-route-
    id="@item.Id">Details</a> |
                <a asp-action="Delete" asp-route-id="@item.Id">Delete</a>
                </td>
                </tr>
            }
        </tbody>
    </table>
```

In the preceding markup, note the `<table>` element's class name is set to `table`. When you run the project and navigate to the products controller (for example, open this view), your table should be styled using the Bootstrap table styles as illustrated in the following screenshot:

Discontinued	Name	Status	UnitPrice	UnitsInStock	
	Chai	Active	18.00	35	Edit | Details | Delete
	Chang	Success	19.00	17	Edit | Details | Delete
	Aniseed Syrup	Info	10.00	13	Edit | Details | Delete
	Pavlova	Warning	17.00	29	Edit | Details | Delete
	Carnarvon Tigers	Danger	62.00	42	Edit | Details | Delete

Product List
Create New

Styling Bootstrap tables

Bootstrap provides additional classes with which you can style your tables to their desired appearance. To inverse the colors of the table, simply change the `<table>` element's class name to `.table table-inverse`. For example, the following table element, `<table class="table table-inverse">`, will produce the following table:

You also have the option to change the appearance of the table's header `<thead>` element to a lighter or darker color. Changing the `<thead>` element's class to `.thead-inverse` will result in the header using the current Bootstrap theme's inverse color (which, in the case of the default Bootstrap style, is darker).

To use the Bootstrap theme's default color for the table heading, simply set the `<thead>` element's class name to `.thead-default`, which will result in a table with a header using the Bootstrap theme's default color, which, in the case of the default Bootstrap theme, is a light gray color, as shown here:

Product List					
Create New					
Discontinued	**Name**	**Status**	**UnitPrice**	**UnitsInStock**	
	Chai	Active	18.00	35	Edit | Details | Delete
	Chang	Success	19.00	17	Edit | Details | Delete
	Aniseed Syrup	Info	10.00	13	Edit | Details | Delete
	Pavlova	Warning	17.00	29	Edit | Details | Delete
	Carnarvon Tigers	Danger	62.00	42	Edit | Details | Delete

To create a bordered table, add `.table-bordered` to its class name, for example:

```
<table class="table table-bordered">
```

To create a table where each odd row is highlighted with another color than the base color, change the table's class name to `.table table-striped`, as illustrated below:

```
<table class="table table-striped">
```

Lastly, Bootstrap also gives you the option to enable hover state on a table. This means the row that the user hovers their cursor over will be highlighted. To accomplish this, change the table class to `.table table-hover`, for example:

```
<table class="table table-hover">
```

All the different class names can be combined to create a zebra-striped, bordered table with hovering, as illustrated in the following markup:

```
<table class="table table-striped table-bordered table-hover">
```

The result will look similar to the following in your browser:

Product List

Create New

Discontinued	Name	Status	UnitPrice	UnitsInStock	
	Chai	Active	18.00	35	Edit	Details	Delete
	Chang	Success	19.00	17	Edit	Details	Delete
	Aniseed Syrup	Info	10.00	13	Edit	Details	Delete
	Pavlova	Warning	17.00	29	Edit	Details	Delete
	Carnarvon Tigers	Danger	62.00	42	Edit	Details	Delete

> You can read more about Bootstrap tables at `http://v4-alpha.getboots trap.com/content/tables/`.

Bootstrap contextual table classes

Bootstrap provides additional classes with which you can style either your table's rows or cells. Adding one of the following class names to either the `<td>` or `<tr>` element of your HTML table will highlight it in either grey, green, blue, orange, or red. These colors respectively represent the following:

- `.table-active`
- `.table-success`
- `.table-info`
- `.table-warning`
- `.table-danger`

Of course, you could also apply these styles dynamically to your MVC views. The
ProductModel class has a Status property, which could be one of the five contextual
Bootstrap classes. By setting the <tr> element's class to this property, the color of the rows
in the table can be dynamically changed based on their data, as illustrated in the following
markup:

```
<tbody>
    @foreach (var item in Model)
    {
        <tr class="table-@item.Status">
            <td>
                @Html.DisplayFor(modelItem => item.Discontinued)
            </td>
            <td>
                @Html.DisplayFor(modelItem => item.Name)
            </td>
            <td>
                @Html.DisplayFor(modelItem => item.Status)
            </td>
            <td>
                @Html.DisplayFor(modelItem => item.UnitPrice)
            </td>
            <td>
                @Html.DisplayFor(modelItem => item.UnitsInStock)
            </td>
            <td>
                <a asp-action="Edit" asp-route-id="@item.Id">Edit</a> |
                <a asp-action="Details" asp-route-id="@item.Id">Details</a>

                <a asp-action="Delete" asp-route-id="@item.Id">Delete</a>
            </td>
        </tr>
    }
</tbody>
```

In the preceding code, you will notice that the table row's class was set to `table-@item.status`. This will cause the rows to be highlighted based on the mapping we've specified for the `status` property, as illustrated in the following screenshot:

Product List					
Create New					
Discontinued	Name	Status	UnitPrice	UnitsInStock	
	Chai	active	18.00	35	Edit | Details | Delete
	Chang	success	19.00	17	Edit | Details | Delete
	Aniseed Syrup	info	10.00	13	Edit | Details | Delete
	Pavlova	warning	17.00	29	Edit | Details | Delete
	Carnarvon Tigers	danger	62.00	42	Edit | Details | Delete

Responsive and smaller tables

To create a smaller table whose cell padding is halved, set the `<table>` element's class to `.table table-sm` as illustrated in the following code snippet:

```
<table class="table table-sm">
```

To change tables into responsive tables that scroll horizontally on small devices, set the `<table>` element's class to `.table table-responsive`, for example:

```
<table class="table table-responsive">
```

The change will only be visible on devices with a resolution smaller than 768 pixels, but no difference will be visible on larger displays.

Bootstrap buttons

Bootstrap provides a wide range of buttons that come in a variety of colors and sizes. The core buttons offer a choice of five colors and four sizes. The color and size of a button are applied using its `class` attribute. Here is the list of classes for setting the size of the button:

- `btn btn-default btn-xs`
- `btn btn-default btn-sm`
- `btn btn-default`
- `btn btn-default btn-lg`

To create four white/default buttons ranging from extra small to large, you'll need to implement the following HTML markup:

```
<div class="row">
    <!-- Standard button -->
    <button type="button" class="btn btn-default btn-xs">Default Extra
Small</button>
    <button type="button" class="btn btn-default btn-sm">Default
Small</button>
    <button type="button" class="btn btn-default">Default</button>
    <button type="button" class="btn btn-default btn-lg">Default
Large</button>
</div>
```

Button colors are also specified by class name. The following is a list of available color class names:

- `btn-default`
- `btn-primary`
- `btn-success`
- `btn-info`
- `btn-warning`

The range of buttons is illustrated in the following screenshot:

Outline buttons

Bootstrap 4 introduces a new style of button called Outline Buttons. To apply it to your buttons, simply add the `.btn-*-outline` class to the `<button>` element. For example, the following code creates a primary (blue) outline button:

```
<button type="button" class="btn btn-primary-outline">Primary</button>
```

The preceding code will generate the following Bootstrap button:

Form layout and elements

Forms make up a large section of most line-of-business applications, and therefore, applying a uniform style to all forms in your web application is not only visually pleasing but also provides your users with a friendlier interface. Bootstrap provides a range of CSS styles to enable you to create visually appealing forms.

Vertical/basic forms

The basic form in Bootstrap always displays its contents in a vertical manner, which means that labels for form <input> elements are displayed above them. With Bootstrap 4, the <fieldset> elements do not have any borders, padding, or margins, and they can be used to wrap inputs into groups by setting the <fieldset> element's class to .form-group. Form elements can also be grouped by placing them inside a <div> element with a class of .form-group.

In the HTML markup that follows, a HTML form will be created using the new ASP.NET Core Tag Helpers containing two Bootstrap form input elements and a submit button. Notice that two form groups are created, one using a <fieldset> element and the other a <div> element:

```
<div class="container">

    <form asp-controller="Account" asp-action="Login" method="post">

        <fieldset class="form-group">
            <label asp-for="Username">Username</label>
            <input asp-for="Username" class="form-control" placeholder=
            "Enter your username"/>
        </fieldset>


        <div class="form-group">
            <label asp-for="Password">Password</label>
            <input asp-for="Password" class="form-control" placeholder=
            "Enter your password"/>
        </div>
        <button type="submit" class="btn btn-primary">Submit</button>

    </form>

</div>
```

The form will look like the following screenshot in your browser:

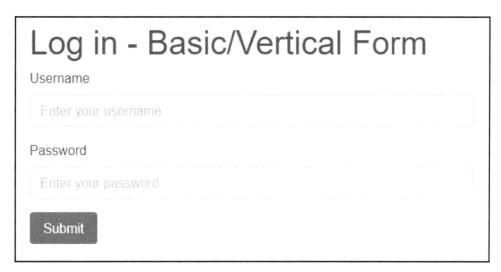

Inline forms

Inline forms are forms whose elements are aligned next to each other. Inline forms will only work on devices with viewports that have a width higher or equal to 768 px. It is good practice to always include labels for your form elements in order for screen readers to be able to read your forms.

If you wish to hide the labels for your form elements, set its label's class to .sr-only. In the following code, we'll use the login form and set its <form> element's class to .form-inline. Also note the labels are not visible, because of their .sr-only class names:

```
<div class="container">

    <h1>Log in - Basic/Vertical Form</h1>

    <form asp-controller="Account" asp-action="Login" method="post">

        <fieldset class="form-group">
            <label asp-for="Username">Username</label>
            <input asp-for="Username" class="form control" placeholder=
            "Enter your username"/>
        </fieldset>


        <div class="form-group">
```

```
            <label asp-for="Password">Password</label>
            <input asp-for="Password" class="form-control" placeholder=
            "Enter your password"/>
        </div>
        <button type="submit" class="btn btn-primary">Submit</button>

    </form>

</div>
```

This will render the following form in your browser:

Grid-based forms

If you need more control over the layout of your Bootstrap forms, you can use the predefined grid classes. With Bootstrap 3, if you wanted to create a horizontal form, you would've given the <form> tag a class name of .form-horizontal. In order to create a horizontal Bootstrap 4 form, you'll need to add the .row class to the .form-group<div> or <fieldset> elements and use the .col-* class name to specify the form control and label sizes.

To vertically align a form component's label, set the label's class to .form-control-label. In the following code, the same login form as before is created as a horizontally aligned form:

```
<div class="container">

    <h1>Log in - Horizontal/Grid Form</h1>

    <form asp-controller="Account" asp-action="Login" method="post">

        <fieldset class="form-group row">
            <label asp-for="Username" class="col-sm-3 form-control-label">
            Username</label>
            <div class="col-sm-9">
```

```
            <input asp-for="Username" class="form-control"
             placeholder="Enter your username" />
        </div>
    </fieldset>

    <div class="form-group row">
        <label asp-for="Password" class="col-sm-3 form-control-label">
         Password</label>
        <div class="col-sm-9">
            <input asp-for="Password" class="form-control"
             placeholder="Enter your password" />
        </div>
    </div>
    <button type="submit" class="btn btn-primary">Submit</button>

</form>

</div>
```

The resulting HTML form will look similar to the following screenshot:

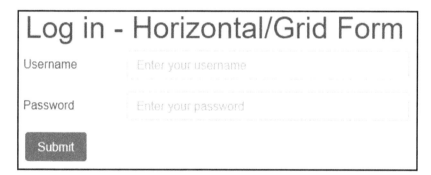

Bootstrap images

Images can be made responsive by setting their class attribute to `.img-fluid`. This will scale the image in relation to its parent element by setting its maximum width to 100% and height to auto.

You also have the option to shape images with either rounded corners, circles, or with an outer border. This is accomplished by setting the `<img>` element's class to one of the following Bootstrap classes:

- `img-rounded`
- `img-circle`
- `img-thumbnail`

In the following image, we've displayed a list of employees, and their pictures. The list of employees could be retrieved from a database and passed to the view:

Employees

Nancy Davolio Sales Representative

Education includes a BA in psychology from Colorado State University in 1970. She also completed 'The Art of the Cold Call.' Nancy is a member of Toastmasters International.

Andrew Fuller Vice President, Sales

Andrew received his BTS commercial in 1974 and a Ph.D. in international marketing from the University of Dallas in 1981. He is fluent in French and Italian and reads German.

Janet Leverling Sales Representative

Janet has a BS degree in chemistry from Boston College (1984). She has also completed a certificate program in food retailing management. Janet was promoted to sales representative in February 1992.

The code that achieves the preceding result, which can be viewed in the accompanying sample project for this chapter, is as follows:

```
@model IEnumerable<Chapter2.Models.EmployeeViewModel>
<div class="container">
    <h2>Employees</h2>

    <div class="row">
        @foreach (var item in Model)
        {
            <div class="col-md-4">
                <img src="@Url.Content("~/img/employees/" + item.Id +
                    ".png")"
```

```
            alt="@item.Name" class="img-circle img-responsive">
        <h3>
            @item.Name<small> @item.JobTitle</small>
        </h3>
        <p>@item.About</p>
    </div>
        }
    </div>

</div>
```

In the preceding code, we looped through each employee item in the model and rendered an <img> element using the Id property as the filename. Each <img> element's class attribute was set to .img-circle that drew the image as a circle.

Bootstrap figures

If you need to display an image or a piece of content with a caption, the <figure> element can be used. The <figure> element is part of the HTML5 spec and is not specific to Bootstrap 4. Bootstrap 4 does, however, provide some helper classes to style the <figure> element appropriately.

For example, the following HTML markup will create a <figure> element containing an image and a caption:

```
<div class="row">
    <div class="col-md-12">
        <figure class="figure">
            <img src="@Url.Content("~/img/bulb.png")" class="figure-img
             img-fluid img-rounded" alt="Light bulb">
            <figcaption class="figure-caption">
                This is a public domain image, available from
            <code>http://publicdomainarchive.com</code>
            </figcaption>
        </figure>
    </div>
</div>
```

The result of the preceding markup, in your browser, will be similar to the following screenshot:

Summary

In this chapter, you've explored how to lay out various elements using the Bootstrap grid and form classes. You've also seen how to enable MVC scaffolding and how to incorporate responsive Bootstrap images and figures in our project.

In the next chapter, you'll discover the various Bootstrap components, including the Bootstrap navigation bar, input groups, progress bars, and alerts, and how to implement them in your ASP.NET MVC project.

3
Using Bootstrap Components

Bootstrap provides over a dozen components, such as input groups, drop-down menus, navigation, alerts, and iconography. By using these components in your web application, you can offer a consistent and easy-to-use interface for your users.

Bootstrap components are essentially made by combining various existing Bootstrap elements, adding a number of unique class names, and representing a number of the common metaphors used on many websites.

In this chapter, we will cover the following topics:

- Using the Bootstrap navigation bar
- How to implement button groups and drop-down menus
- Exploring the different input groups
- Using the different Navs (navbars, pills, and so on)
- Implementing alerts, progress bars, and badges
- Introduction to cards

The Bootstrap navigation bar

The Bootstrap navigation bar is one of the components that is used on the majority of sites using the Bootstrap framework. The navbar functions as a navigation header in your sites and will collapse on smaller devices showing only an icon menu, using the Bootstrap Collapse plugin. It is ideally suited to include site branding and navigation.

Basic navbar

A basic navigation bar consists of the website logo or brand name, navigation menu, and options for toggling behavior on smaller devices. A basic Bootstrap navigation bar might look similar to this:

The preceding navigation bar consists of an <a> element containing the site logo, with a class name of .navbar-brand. It also contains a <ul> element, whose class name is set to .nav navbar-nav. Each <li> child element's class name is set to .nav-item. The full HTML markup required to create the navigation bar is listed here:

```
<nav class="navbar navbar-full navbar-dark bg-primary">
    <a class="navbar-brand" href="#">
        <img src="~/img/bootstraplogo.png" alt="Logo"/>
    </a>
    <ul class="nav navbar-nav">
        <li class="nav-item active">
            <a class="nav-link" asp-controller="Home"
            asp-action="Index">Home</a>
        </li>
        <li class="nav-item">
            <a class="nav-link" href="#">About</a>
        </li>
        <li class="nav-item">
            <a class="nav-link" href="#">Products</a>
        </li>
        <li class="nav-item">
            <a class="nav-link" href="#">Contact</a>
        </li>
    </ul>
</nav>
```

Responsive navbar

Bootstrap uses the Collapse library to allow navigation bars to be responsive on smaller devices. You may have noticed a hamburger menu that hides the menu item that is normally visible when visiting most modern websites from your mobile device:

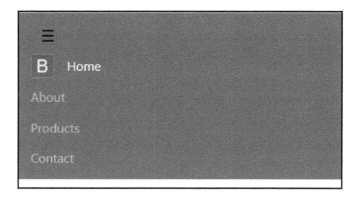

In order to achieve the desired menu illustrated in the previous screenshot, you'll need to change the navbar markup to the following:

```
<nav class="navbar navbar-full navbar-dark bg-primary">
    <button class="navbar-toggler hidden-sm-up" type="button" data-
toggle="collapse" data-target="#navCollapse">
        ≡
    </button>
    <div class="collapse navbar-toggleable-xs" id="navCollapse">
        <a class="navbar-brand" href="#">
            <img src="~/img/bootstraplogo.png" alt="Logo" />
        </a>
        <ul class="nav navbar-nav">
            <li class="nav-item active">
                <a class="nav-link" asp-controller="Home"
                 asp-action="Index">Home</a>
            </li>
            <li class="nav-item">
                <a class="nav-link" href="#">About</a>
            </li>
            <li class="nav-item">
                <a class="nav-link" href="#">Products</a>
            </li>
            <li class="nav-item">
                <a class="nav-link" href="#">Contact</a>
            </li>
        </ul>
    </div>
</nav>
```

As highlighted in the preceding code, and in order to show a button that will toggle the navigation bar items when collapsed, a `<button>` element was added with a class name of `.navbar-toggler hidden-sm-up`.

Note that the icon displayed on the button is a Font Awesome icon, and will only work if you've added Font Awesome to your project as explained in `Chapter 1`, *Getting started with ASP.NET Core and Bootstrap 4.*

The rest of the menu items are wrapped inside a `<div>` element with a class name of `.collapse navbar-toggleable-xs`.

By combining the `.navbar-toggler` and `.navbar-toggleable-*` class names you can specify on which device sizes the content is meant to be shown.

> Rest assured that the Bootstrap team is actively working on improving and enhancing all of Bootstrap, and most of the problems should be sorted out as soon as the final version of Bootstrap 4 is released. You can see a list of open issues for Bootstrap 4 on GitHub `https://github.com/twbs/bootstrap/issues/`.

Navbar with dropdown menus

In many instances, you would like to display additional child menus under the main menu items. For example, in the following screenshot, we display a list of product categories as child menus of the Product menu:

The preceding navigation bar is created with the same markup as the first nav bar, but the Products menu item's class name is changed to `.nav item dropdown` and the `<a>` element inside the `<li>` element receives a class name of `. nav-link dropdown-toggle`. The HTML markup for the Products menu item is as follows:

```
<li class="nav-item dropdown">
    <a class="nav-link dropdown-toggle" data-toggle="dropdown"  href="#"
role="button"
        aria-haspopup="true" aria-expanded="false">
        Products
    </a>
    <div class="dropdown-menu" aria-labelledby="Products">
        <a class="dropdown-item" href="#">Beverages</a>
        <a class="dropdown-item" href="#">Condiments</a>
        <a class="dropdown-item" href="#">Seafood</a>
    </div>
</li>
```

Navbar color schemes

Bootstrap 4 allows you to theme the navbar with a simple combination of the `.navbar-*` and `.bg-*` class names of the `<nav>` element. For example, in the following screenshot, we created two navigation bars, one with a blue and the other with a red background:

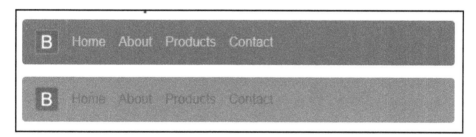

The preceding navbar colors are achieved by adding `.bg-primary` or `.bg-danger` to the navbar `<nav>` element.

```
<nav class="navbar navbar-dark bg-primary">
<nav class="navbar navbar-light bg-danger">
```

You can also apply a custom color to a navbar by setting the `background-color` CSS attribute. For example, the following screenshot was achieved by using the following HTML markup:

```
<nav class="navbar navbar-light bg-inverse" style="background-color:
#8361B7;">
```

Bootstrap provide four basic color styles that you can use to style the navbar:

- `bg-success` - Green
- `bg-warning` - Orange
- `bg-info` - Light Blue
- `bg-danger` - Red

List groups

List groups are flexible components that either display simple lists of elements or can be combined with other elements to create complex lists with custom content. As an example, we'll create a sample search page that will display the search results in a Bootstrap list group.

Start by completing the following steps:

1. Add a new controller called `SearchController.cs` to your project.

2. Change the `Index` action to the following:

```
public IActionResult Index(string query)
{
    ViewBag.SearchQuery = query;
    var products = GetProducts();
    if (!string.IsNullOrEmpty(query))
    {
      var results = products.Where(p => p.Name.Contains(query));
      return View(results);
    }
    return View(products);
}
```

3. The preceding code retrieves a list of all products using the `GetProducts` method. It will then filter the list of products if the `query` parameter contains a value and returns the results. If the query parameter does not contain any value, it will return all the products.

4. The code for the `GetProducts` method is as follows:

```
private List<ProductModel> GetProducts()
{
    var model = new List<ProductModel>();
    var product1 = new ProductModel { Name = "Chai", UnitPrice =
18,
    UnitsInStock = 35, Discontinued = false, Id = 1,
    Status = "active" };
    var product2 = new ProductModel { Name = "Chang", UnitPrice =
19,
    UnitsInStock = 17, Discontinued = false, Id = 2,
    Status = "success" };
    var product3 = new ProductModel { Name = "Aniseed Syrup",
UnitPrice
    = 10, UnitsInStock = 13, Discontinued = false, Id = 3,
    Status = "info" };
    var product4 = new ProductModel { Name = "Pavlova", UnitPrice =
17,
    UnitsInStock = 29, Discontinued = false, Id = 4,
    Status = "warning" };
    var product5 = new ProductModel { Name = "Carnarvon Tigers",
    UnitPrice = 62, UnitsInStock = 42, Discontinued = true, Id = 5,
    Status = "danger" };
    model.AddRange(new[]
    { product1, product2, product3, product4, product5 });
    return model;
}
```

5. Next, create a new subfolder in the `Views` folder called `Search` and add a new view called `Index.cshtml` to it.

6. Change the view's HTML to the following:

```
@model IEnumerable<Chapter3.Models.ProductModel>
<div class="container" style="padding-top: 30px;">
  <h1>
  Product search results
  <small>
  @if (ViewBag.SearchQuery != null)
  {<text>Results for your search term: </text>
@ViewBag.SearchQuery
  }
```

```
   </small>
   </h1>
   <ul class="list-group">
   @foreach (var item in Model)
    {
      <li class="list-group-item">
      <span class="label label-default label-pill pull-xs-right">
        @item.UnitsInStock</span>
        @item.Name
      </li>
    }
   </ul>
   </div>
```

7. In the preceding markup, the product items are loaded into an unordered list element `<ul>` as anchor `<li>` elements. Each `<li>` element's class name should be set to `.list-group-item`. The view should look like the following screenshot inside your browser:

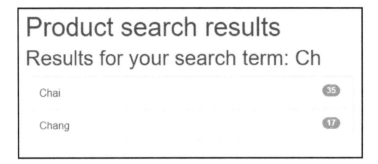

Badges

Badges are used to highlight items. You would normally see badges to indicate the number of new or unread items depending on the type of application. We used badges on the product search result page to indicate the number of units currently in stock:

```
<li class="list-group-item">
    <span class="tag tag-default tag-pill pull-xs-
right">@item.UnitsInStock</span>
    @item.Name
</li>
```

Adding a badge to an element is as simple as adding a `<span>` element and setting its class name to `.tag`. You'll also notice that you can set the color of the badge using the default Bootstrap context classes. For example, to change the badge color to red, change the `.tag-default` class name to `.tag-danger`.

Media object

The media object component can be used to build hierarchical style lists such as blog comments or tweets. In the following example application, we'll use it to return a search result view when the user searches for employees. Our model will have a `'ReportsTo'` field indicating which employee other employees report to; the media object component would be ideal to indicate this visually.

The method located in `SearchController` that searches for the employees and returns the results to the view is as follows:

```
public IActionResult SearchEmployees(string query)
{
    ViewBag.SearchQuery = query;
    var employees = GetEmployees();
    if (!string.IsNullOrEmpty(query))
    {
        var results = employees.Where(p => p.Name.Contains(query));
        return View(results);
    }
    return View(employees);
}
```

The preceding code will retrieve a list of employees using the `GetEmployees` method and, if the query parameter is not empty, return employees matching the search criteria and pass all employees to the view.

The code for the `GetEmployees` method is as follows:

```
private List<EmployeeViewModel> GetEmployees()
{
    var vicePresident = new EmployeeViewModel
    {
        Id = 2,
        Name = "Andrew Fuller",
        JobTitle = "Vice President, Sales",
        ReportsTo = null
    };
```

```
        var reportingEmployees = new List<EmployeeViewModel>
        {
            new EmployeeViewModel { Id = 1, Name = "Nancy Davolio",JobTitle =
            "Sales Representative", ReportsTo = 2},
            new EmployeeViewModel { Id = 3, Name = "Janet Leverling", JobTitle
=
            "Sales Representative", ReportsTo = 2 },
            new EmployeeViewModel { Id = 4, Name = "Laura Callahan", JobTitle =
            "Inside Sales Coordinator", ReportsTo = 2 }
        };

        vicePresident.ReportingEmployees = reportingEmployees;
        var employees = new List<EmployeeViewModel> { vicePresident };

        return employees;
    }
```

The view for the employees search result uses the media object component to style the employee information and display the employee photos. The markup for the view is as follows:

```
@model IEnumerable<Chapter3.Models.EmployeeViewModel>
<div class="container">
        <h1>
            Employees Results <small>Results for your search term:
            "@ViewBag.SearchQuery"</small>
        </h1>
    @foreach (var item in Model)
    {
        <div class="media">
            <div class="media-left">
                <a href="#">
                    <img class="media-object" src="@Url.Content("~/img
                    /employees/" + @item.Id + ".png")" alt="@item.Name"
                    width="64" height="64">
                </a>
            </div>
            <div class="media-body">
                <h4 class="media-heading">@item.Name</h4>
                @item.About
                @foreach (var emp in @item.ReportingEmployees)
                {
                    <div class="media">
                        <a class="media-left" href="#">
                            <img class="media-object"
src="@Url.Content("~/img
                            /employees/" + @emp.Id + ".png")"
alt="@emp.Name"
```

```
                width="64" height="64">
        </a>
        <div class="media-body">
            <h4 class="media-heading">@emp.Name</h4>
            @emp.JobTitle
        </div>
    </div>
}
    </div>
    </div>
}
</div>
```

The media object component is built up using a combination of elements with the class names of .media, media-heading, and media-body. The .media-object class name is used to indicate media objects such as images, video, or audio. The resulting view should look similar to the following screenshot:

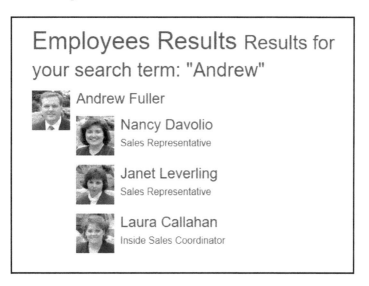

Breadcrumbs

Breadcrumbs are a common metaphor used in web design to indicate to the user what their current location is inside a navigation tree. It is similar to a file path inside Windows Explorer. Breadcrumbs are ideal for a site with many sub-navigation levels, and they allow the user to navigate between the various parent and child pages.

In the following markup, we'll use a combination of Razor and HTML to build a breadcrumb component with which the user can navigate back to the Home page or the Manage page:

```
<ol class="breadcrumb">
    <li class="breadcrumb-item"><a href="#">Home</a></li>
    <li class="breadcrumb-item"><a href="#">Search</a></li>
    <li class="breadcrumb-item active">Employees</li>
</ol>
```

The preceding markup contains an ordered list <ol> element with a class name of .breadcrumb. Each child element of the breadcrumb is added as a list item <li> element with a class name of .breadcrumb-item. To indicate to the user that the last level of the breadcrumb is the active page, we set its <li> element's class name to .active. The result of the preceding code will look like the following screenshot when visiting the page:

Home / Search / Employees

Pagination

Pagination is used to divide content, usually lists, into separate pages. For example, when scaffolding a List view, the default scaffolding template generates a table that contains a row for each item in the collection you pass into the view. This is fine for small amounts of data, but if the list contains hundreds of items, your page will take a very long time to load. Ideally, you would like to split your list view into a manageable 5 to 10 items per page view.

In the first edition of this book we used the PagedList.Mvc NuGet package to make paging using Bootstrap 3 easier. This package is no longer maintained, but there is a drop-in replacement library available on NuGet called X.PagedList.

Unfortunately, neither NuGet Packages would work, because of their dependencies on System.Web, which was removed from ASP.NET Core. In the following example we'll use an open source library called cloudscribe.Web.Pagination to create a paged list using Bootstrap 4.

To create the paged list, follow these steps:

1. Open the `project.json` file, and add the following to the dependencies section:
   `"cloudscribe.Web.Pagination": "1.0.2-*"` Visual Studio will download
   the required dependencies. Next, open the `ProductController.cs` class file,
   add a new action called `Index`, and change its code to the following:

```
public IActionResult Index(int? page)
{
    int pageSize = 10;
    var currentPageNum = page.HasValue ? page.Value : 1;
    var offset = (pageSize * currentPageNum) - pageSize;
    var model = new ProductPagingViewModel();
    model.Products = GetProducts()
    .Skip(offset)
    .Take(pageSize).OrderBy(p=>p.Name)
    .ToList();
    model.Paging.CurrentPage = currentPageNum;
    model.Paging.ItemsPerPage = pageSize;
    model.Paging.TotalItems = GetProducts().Count;
    return View(model);
}
```

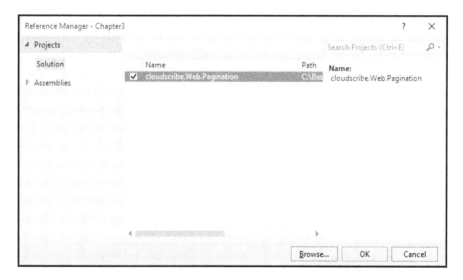

In the preceding code, a new action method called `Index` was created that
accepts an integer parameter called `page`. This parameter is used to indicate
which page of the list the user is currently viewing. A list of products is
retrieved and ordered by the `Name` property.

The `pageSize` variable is used to set the number of items each page should display. The list of products is then returned as a `ProductPagingViewModel`. The code for the `ProductPaginViewModel` is as follows:

```
public class ProductPagingViewModel
{
  public ProductPagingViewModel()
  {
      Paging = new PaginationSettings();
  }

  public string Query { get; set; } = string.Empty;

  public List<ProductModel> Products { get; set; } = null;

  public PaginationSettings Paging { get; set; }
}
```

2. Next, open the `Startup.cs` file and add the following code to the `ConfigureServices` method:

```
services.AddCloudscribePagination();
```

   If the project's `View` folder does not already contain a `_ViewImports.cshtml` file, add it and change its content to the following:

```
@addTagHelper *, Microsoft.AspNetCore.Mvc.TagHelpers
@addTagHelper "*, cloudscribe.Web.Pagination"
```

3. You need to add the preceding code, because `TagHelpers` are opt-in. `TagHelpers` are discussed in Chapter 5, *Creating MVC Bootstrap Helper and Tag Helpers*.
4. Add a new view, called `Index.cshtml`, to the `Views\Product` folder.
5. Add the following to the `Index.cshtml` file:

```
@model Chapter3.Models.ProductPagingViewModel

<div class="container" style="padding-top: 10px;">
    <h1>
        Products
    </h1>

    <table class="table table-striped table-bordered">
        <thead>
        <tr>
```

```
            <th>
                Product Name
            </th>
            <th>
                Unit Price
            </th>
            <th>
                Units in Stock
            </th>
            <th>
                Discontinued
            </th>
        </tr>
        </thead>
        <tbody>
        @foreach (var item in Model.Products)
        {
            <tr class="@item.Status">
                <td>@item.Name</td>
                <td>@item.UnitPrice</td>
                <td>@item.UnitsInStock</td>
                <td>@item.Discontinued</td>
            </tr>}
        </tbody>
    </table>
    <div>
        <cs-pager cs-paging-pagesize="@Model.Paging.ItemsPerPage"
                  cs-paging-pagenumber="@Model.Paging.CurrentPage"
                  cs-paging-totalitems="@Model.Paging.TotalItems"
                  cs-pagenumber-param="page"
                  cs-show-first-last="true"
                  cs-suppress-empty-nextprev="true"
                  cs-suppress-inactive-firstlast="true"
                  cs-first-page-text="First"
                  cs-last-page-text="Last"
                  cs-pager-li-current-class="active"
                  cs-pager-li-non-active-class="disabled">
        </cs-pager>
    </div>
</div>
```

In the preceding HTML/Razor markup, the model for the view is declared as a `ProductPaginViewModel` object containing a list of `ProductModel` objects.

At the bottom of the `<table>` element a custom `TagHelper` is used to render the paging for the table. The `TagHelper` is part of the `cloudscribe.Web.Pagination` library added earlier.

The `cloudscribe.Web.Pagination` library was created to support Bootstrap 3. In order for it to work with Bootstrap 4, you can change the source code of the library directly by following these steps:

1. Open the `PagerTagHelper.cs` file, located inside the `cloudscribe.Web.Pagination` project in the Visual Studio Solution Explorer.
2. Locate the following line inside the `Process` method. It should be at line number 211:

    ```
    var li = new TagBuilder("li");
    ```

3. The Bootstrap 4 pagination component requires its `<li>` elements to have a class name of `.page-link`. Change this by adding the following line below the line mentioned in the previous step:

    ```
    li.AddCssClass("page-item");
    ```

4. Bootstrap 4 also requires that `<a>` elements used for pagination have a class name of `.page-link`. In order to make the `PagerTagHelper` work with Bootstrap 4, change the following code in the `Process` method (line 224):

    ```
    var a = new TagBuilder("a");
    a.AddCssClass("page-link");
    ```

5. You do not need to change the source code of the `Cloudscribe.Web.Pagination` library, you can also achieve the correct Bootstrap 4 styling for the pagination component by adding the following JavaScript code to your page:

    ```
    $(document).ready(function () {
        $('ul.pagination > li').addClass('page-item');
        $('li.page-item > a').addClass('page-link');
        $('li.active').empty();
        $('li.active').append('<a class="page-link" href="#">' +
            @Model.Paging.CurrentPage + ' <span class="sr-
    only">(current)</span>
        </a>');
    });
    ```

All that is left to do is to build the project and open the page action of the product controller in your browser. You should see a paged table with a Bootstrap 4 styled pagination component divided into pages containing five products each:

Product Name	Unit Price	Units In Stock	Discontinued
Aniseed Syrup	10.00	13	
Carnarvon Tigers	62.00	42	
Chai	18.00	35	
Chang	19.00	17	
Chef Anton's Cajun Seasoning	22.00	53	

Input groups

Input groups are another way to provide the user with additional information about the data you expect them to enter in a specific form element. Bootstrap provides classes to add sections either before or after an input element. These sections can contain either text or an icon.

To create a text input element to indicate to the user that we require them to enter a phone number into the field, we'll use the following markup:

```
@model Chapter3.Models.PersonModel
<div class="container">
    <div class="row">
        <div class="col-md-6">
            <label asp-for="Phonenumber" class="col-md-4 control-label">
            </label>
            <div class="input-group">
```

```
                <span class="input-group-addon" id="PhoneNumber">
                <i class="fa fa-phone"></i></span>
                <input asp-for="Phonenumber" class="form-control"
                 placeholder="Phone number"/>
            </div>
        </div>
    </div>
</div>
```

The result of the preceding markup will be a text input element with a gray section to its left with an image of a telephone inside it, as illustrated in the following image:

Font Awesome is not included in the Bootstrap 4 distribution. Chapter 1, *Getting Started with ASP.NET Core and Bootstrap 4*, details how you can add it to your project.

You can also create input groups that are aligned on the right-hand side of text inputs and that contain text instead of images. For example, the following markup creates a text input field that indicates to the user that only the first part of an e-mail address is required and that the last part will automatically be appended:

```
<div class="row">
    <div class="col-md-6">
        <label asp-for="Email" class="col-md-4 control-label"></label>
        <div class="input-group">
            <input asp-for="Email" class="form-control" placeholder="Email
             address" />
            <span class="input-group-addon"
id="Email">@@northwind.com</span>
        </div>
    </div>
</div>
```

The result of the preceding markup will look like the following image inside your browser:

You can also create a text input with a gray section on both sides with the following code:

```
<div class="row">
    <div class="col-md-6">
        <label asp-for="Salary" class="col-md-4 control-label"></label>
        <div class="input-group">
            <span class="input-group-addon">$</span>
            <input type="text" class="form-control">
            <span class="input-group-addon">.00</span>
        </div>
    </div>
</div>
```

In the preceding code, we created a text input with a gray section with a dollar sign on the left side and a gray section on the right containing .00. This will indicate to the user that we expect a round number and that the system always expects zero decimals:

Button dropdowns

Button dropdowns are useful when you need a button that can perform multiple related actions. For example, you could have a save button that saves a record, but you would also like to give the user an option to save the record and automatically show a new empty form to create another record. This will be beneficial to the user when they need to create multiple records of the same type.

For example, the following code creates a button dropdown menu inside a form that will create a save button with two additional actions:

```
<div class="dropdown">
    <button class="btn btn-primary dropdown-toggle" type="button"
     data-toggle="dropdown" aria-haspopup="true" aria-expanded="false">
        Save
    </button>
    <div class="dropdown-menu" aria-labelledby="dropdownMenu2">
        <button class="dropdown-item" type="submit">Save &amp; New</button>
        <div class="dropdown-divider"></div>
        <button class="dropdown-item" type="button">Duplicate</button>
    </div>
</div>
```

The result will look like the following inside your browser:

Alerts

The alert component is used to provide visual feedback to the user. This can be used to provide the user with either confirmation messages that a record has been saved, warning messages that an error has occurred, or an information message based on a system event.

Bootstrap provides four differently styled alerts. For instance, the following markup generates green, blue, orange, and red alert boxes:

```
<div class="alert alert-success" role="alert">
    <strong>Success!</strong> You have successfully saved the file.
</div>
<div class="alert alert-info" role="alert">
    <strong>Info.</strong> Something has just happened.
</div>
<div class="alert alert-warning" role="alert">
    <strong>Warning!</strong> The file size is too big.
</div>
<div class="alert alert-danger" role="alert">
    <strong>Danger!</strong> The file could not be saved
</div>
```

The alert boxes should look similar to the following image in your browser:

Success! You have successfully saved the file.

Info. Something has just happened.

Warning! The file size is too big

Danger! The file could not be saved

A dismissible alert is an alert that can be closed by the user clicking on a small *X* icon in its top right-hand corner. In order to create a dismissible alert, you must have the alert plugin or the Bootstrap JavaScript library loaded, added the .alert-dismissable class name to the alert <div>, and set the alert's close button's class to .close. The following HTML markup illustrates how to create a dismissible alert:

```
<div class="alert alert-danger alert-dismissible fade in" role="alert">
    <button type="button" class="close" data-dismiss="alert"
     aria-label="Close">
        <span aria-hidden="true">&times;</span>
    </button>
    <strong>Something went wrong!</strong> You can close this alert when
done.
</div>
```

Progress bars

Progress bars are a metaphor used with traditional desktops as well as web development to provide visual feedback to a user on the progress of a task or action. Bootstrap provides a number of different styled progress bars.

Basic progress bar

The basic Bootstrap progress bar displays a plain blue colored progress bar. Bootstrap 4 uses the HTML 5 `<progress>` element, with a class name of `.progress`, to display progress bars. The following markup generates a basic progress bar with a maximum value of `100` and current value of `50`:

```
<progress class="progress" value="50" max="100"></progress>
```

The result of the markup is shown in the following screenshot:

Contextual progress bars

You can use the same button and alert style classes to generate different colored progress bars. This is accomplished by setting the progress bar's class name to one of the following:

- `progress progress-success`
- `progress progress-info`
- `progress progress-warning`
- `progress progress-danger`

The result is illustrated in the following screenshot:

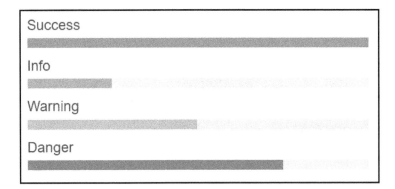

Striped and animated progress bars

To generate progress bars with a gradient striped effect, add the `.progress progress-striped` class name to the `<progress>` element:

```
<progress class="progress progress-striped progress-danger" value="75"
max="100"></progress>
```

The result is shown in the following screenshot:

To add an animated effect that will give the impression that the stripes on the progress bar are moving, simply add a `.progress-animated` class to its parent `<progress>` element:

```
<progress class="progress progress-striped progress-danger progress-
animated" value="75" max="100"></progress>
```

Cards

With Bootstrap 4, wells, panels, and thumbnails have been replaced by cards. A card is a flexible container for many kinds of content. It includes customization options for headers, footers, and colors.

An example of a Bootstrap card component that contains an image, a title, and text content is illustrated in the following screenshot:

The markup required to generate the Bootstrap card is as follows:

```
<div class="card">
    <img class="card-img-top" src="~/img/skyline.jpg" alt="Card image cap">
    <div class="card-block">
        <h4 class="card-title">Chicago Skyline</h4>
        <p class="card-text">Chicago Skyline At Night from Hotel 71 on
Wacker
         Drive.</p>
        <a href="http://publicdomainarchive.com/free-stock-photos-chicago-
         skyline-night-hotel-71-wacker-drive/"
            class="btn btn-primary">Visit Source</a>
    </div>
</div>
```

Summary

In this chapter, we've explored the many different Bootstrap components, as well as how to use them inside your ASP.NET MVC projects. We also looked at external libraries that can help with creating paged lists.

In the next chapter, we'll delve deeper into the Bootstrap components by investigating how to add further interactivity to your site using the Bootstrap JavaScript plugins.

4
Using Bootstrap JavaScript Components

Bootstrap's JavaScript features are all built on top of the jQuery library and either provide completely new functionality or extend the functionality of the existing Bootstrap components.

The plugins can be used by simply adding data attributes to your page elements, but they can also provide a rich programmatic API, if needed.

In this chapter, we will cover the following topics:

- Using dropdown menus and creating a cascading dropdown menu
- How to use modal dialogs
- Separate content inside views with tabs
- How to implement tooltips and popovers
- How to use the accordion component
- Creating a slideshow using the carousel

Data attributes versus the programmatic API

Bootstrap offers the ability to use its plugins entirely through HTML markup. This means that in order to use most of the plugins, you do not need to write a single line of JavaScript. Using data attributes is the recommended approach and should be your first option when using Bootstrap plugins.

For example, to allow an `alert` element to be `dismissible`, you'll add the `data-dismiss="alert"` attribute to either a `button` or anchor element, as illustrated in the following code:

```
<div class="alert alert-danger">
    <button data-dismiss="alert" class="close" type="button">×</button>
    <strong>Warning</strong> Shuttle launch in t-minus 10 seconds.
</div>
```

You also have the option to perform the same action using the programmatic API via JavaScript. The following code uses jQuery to close a specific `alert` element when the user clicks on a button:

```
<button class="close" type="button"
onclick="$('#myalert').alert('close')">×</button>
```

In order to use Bootstrap plugins, you'll need to include the `bootstrap.js` or `bootstrap.min.js` file in your project. This file contains all the Bootstrap plugins, but if you do not intend to use every plugin in your project you can choose to download a custom build. At the time of writing, these include Reboot, Grid only, and Flexbox builds.

Cascading dropdowns

You can add `drop-down` menus to almost any Bootstrap component using the `dropdown` plugin. A cascading `drop-down` menu is a `drop-down` menu that updates its data based on a value selected in another `drop-down` menu. To add cascading `drop-down` menus, perform the following steps:

1. Inside Visual Studio, add a new controller called `DropdownController.cs` to your `Controllers` folder.
2. In the `Index` action, add the following code, which will create a list of managers and load a list of reporting employees for the selected manager:

```
public IActionResult Index(int id = 2)
{
    var managers = new List<EmployeeModel>();
    var vicePresident = new EmployeeModel { Id = 2, Name = "Andrew
    Fuller", JobTitle = "Vice President, Sales", ReportsTo = null
};
    var salesManager = new EmployeeModel { Id = 5, Name =
    "Steven Buchanan", JobTitle = "Sales Manager", ReportsTo = null
};
```

```
        managers.Add(vicePresident);
        managers.Add(salesManager);

        ViewBag.Managers = managers;
        var model = GetEmployees(id);
        return View(model);
    }
```

3. The `GetEmployees` method simply returns an `EmployeeModel` with its child collection of reporting employees. The code for the method is as follows:

```
    private EmployeeModel GetEmployees(int id = 2)
    {
        if (id == 2)
        {
            var vicePresident = new EmployeeModel { Id = 2, Name =
            "Andrew Fuller", JobTitle = "Vice President, Sales",
            ReportsTo = null };
            var vicePresidentEmployees = new List<EmployeeModel>
            {
                new EmployeeModel { Id = 1, Name = "Nancy Davolio",
                JobTitle = "Sales Representative", ReportsTo = 2},
                new EmployeeModel { Id = 3, Name = "Janet Leverling",
                JobTitle = "Sales Representative", ReportsTo = 2 },
                new EmployeeModel { Id = 4, Name = "Laura Callahan",
                JobTitle = "Inside Sales Coordinator", ReportsTo = 2 }
            };
            vicePresident.ReportingEmployees = vicePresidentEmployees;
            return vicePresident;
        }


        var salesManager = new EmployeeModel { Id = 5, Name =
        "Steven Buchanan", JobTitle = "Sales Manager", ReportsTo = null
};
        var salesManagerEmployees = new List<EmployeeModel>
        {
            new EmployeeModel { Id = 1, Name = "Michael Suyama",
            JobTitle = "Sales Representative", ReportsTo = 5 },
            new EmployeeModel { Id = 3, Name = "Robert King",
            JobTitle = "Sales Representative", ReportsTo = 5 },
            new EmployeeModel { Id = 4, Name = "Anne Dodsworth",
            JobTitle = "Inside Sales Coordinator", ReportsTo = 5 }
        };
        salesManager.ReportingEmployees = salesManagerEmployees;

        return salesManager;
    }
```

4. Next, add a new view called `Index.cshtml` to the `Views\Dropdown` folder.

5. The view will only contain two Bootstrap `drop-down` buttons. One will show a list of managers and the other a list of the managers' reporting employees. The list of managers will pass in via the `ViewBag` object and the list of employees will read from the model that will be passed into the view. The HTML markup for the view is as follows:

```
<div class="container">
  <h1 id="heading">Cascading dropdown</h1>
    <form>
      <div class="form-group row">
        <label class="col-sm-2 form-control-label">Manager</label>
          <div class="col-sm-10">
            <div class="btn-group">
              <button type="button" class="btn btn-danger"
               id="selectedManager">@Model.Name</button>
              <button type="button" class="btn btn-danger dropdown-
               toggle" data-toggle="dropdown" aria-haspopup="true"
               aria-expanded="false">
               <span class="sr-only">Toggle Dropdown</span>
              </button>
              <div class="dropdown-menu" id="managerlist">
                @foreach (var manager in ViewBag.Managers)
                {
                    <a class="dropdown-item" href="#"
                    data-id="@manager.Id">@manager.Name</a>
                }
              </div>
            </div>
          </div>
      </div>
      <div class="form-group row">
          <label class="col-sm-2 form-control-label">Employee</label>
          <div class="col-sm-10">
            <div class="btn-group">
              <button type="button" class="btn btn-primary">
               Select Employee</button>
              <button type="button" class="btn btn-primary dropdown-
               toggle" data-toggle="dropdown" aria-haspopup="true"
               aria-expanded="false">
                  <span class="sr-only">Toggle Dropdown</span>
              </button>
              <div class="dropdown-menu" id="employees">
                  @foreach (var employee in Model.ReportingEmployees)
                  {
                      <a class="dropdown-item" href="#"
                       data-id="@employee.Id">@employee.Name</a>
```

```
                }
            </div>
        </div>
    </div>
</div>
    </form>
</div>
```

6. In order to update the employees' `dropdown` button with the list of reporting employees for the selected manager, you will need to add the following JavaScript to the page:

```
<script type="text/javascript">
    $('#managerlist a').on('click', function () {
        var $this = $(this);
        var managerId = $this.data('id');
        $("#selectedManager").text($this.text());

        $.ajax({
            type: 'GET',
            dataType: 'html',
            url: '@Url.Action("GetReportingEmployees",
"Dropdown")',
            data: { id: managerId }
        }).done(function (data) {
            $('#employees').replaceWith(data);
        });
    });
</script>
```

7. The preceding JavaScript will get the ID value of the selected manager via its `data-id` attribute. Next, it will make an AJAX call to the `GetReportingEmployees` action in the `Dropdown` controller.

8. The `GetReportingEmployees` method in the `Dropdown` controller will return a partial view result containing the list of reporting employees. The code for the method is as follows:

```
public PartialViewResult GetReportingEmployees(int id)
{
    var model = GetEmployees(id);
    return PartialView("_employees", model.ReportingEmployees);
}
```

A partial view enables you to render content or a child view inside another or parent view.

9. You would need to add a new partial view to the `Views\Dropdown` folder called `_employees.cshtml` for the preceding code to work. The HTML markup for the view looks as follows:

```
@model IEnumerable<Chapter4.Models.EmployeeModel>
<div class="dropdown-menu" id="employees">
@foreach (var employee in Model)
{
  <a class="dropdown-item" href="#"
  data-id="@employee.Id">@employee.Name</a>
}
</div>
```

10. The preceding HTML/Razor markup loops through the list of employees, passed in via the model, and creates a new `dropdown` button with the data.

The result of the preceding steps should be a view similar to the following screenshot:

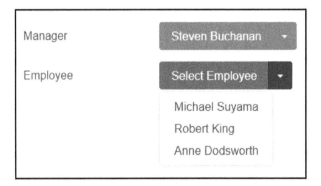

Modal dialogs

Modals are used to provide a pop-up dialog style element that can be used to provide information to the user or even allow the user, to complete a form inside the modal. A Bootstrap modal is essentially made of three parts: a header, body, and footer. You can put any standard HTML markup inside the modal's `body` element, including standard text or even an embedded YouTube video.

As a general rule, always place the modal's markup in a top-level position inside your view, the top or bottom of the view is the best place to put your modal markup.

In order to show a modal when a button is clicked, you can set the `data-toggle` and `data-target` attributes of a Bootstrap button. For example, in the following HTML markup, a button's `data-toggle` attribute has been set to modal and its `data-target` attribute has been set to `employeeModal`:

```
<div class="row">
    <button type="button" class="btn btn-primary btn-lg" data-toggle=
        "modal" data-target="#employeeModal">
        Show Employee Modal
    </button>
</div>
```

The `data-target` attribute should contain the ID of the modal `<div>` element. The `<div>` element that contains the modal should have a class name of `modal`:

```
<div class="modal fade" id="employeeModal" tabindex="-1" role="dialog"
aria-labelledby="Employee Information" aria-hidden="true">
    <div class="modal-dialog" role="document">
        <div class="modal-content">
            <div class="modal-header">
                <button type="button" class="close" data-dismiss=
                 "modal" aria-label="Close">
                    <span aria-hidden="true">&times;</span>
                </button>
                <h4 class="modal-title">Andrew Fuller</h4>
            </div>
            <div class="modal-body">
                <p>
                    Andrew received his BTS commercial in 1974 and a Ph.D.
in international marketing from the University of Dallas in 1981.
                    He is fluent in French and Italian and reads German. He
joined the company as a sales representative, was promoted to sales
                    manager in January 1992 and to vice president of sales
in March 1993. Andrew is a member of the Sales Management Roundtable,
                    the Seattle Chamber of Commerce, and the Pacific Rim
Importers Association.
                </p>
            </div>
            <div class="modal-footer">
                <button type="button" class="btn btn-secondary" data-
dismiss="modal">Close</button>
                <button type="button" class="btn btn-primary">Send
Email</button>
            </div>
```

```
          </div>
      </div>
  </div>
```

The result of the preceding HTML markup should look similar to the following screenshot:

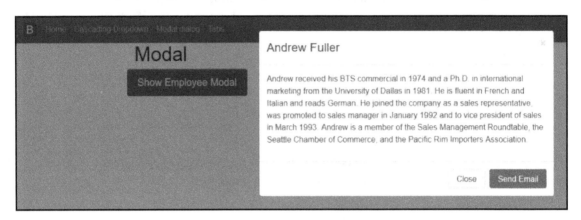

Modal size and animation

Bootstrap modals have three standard sizes. If you would like to have a large modal or small modal, add the `.modal-lg` or `.modal-sm` class name to the `<div>` element with the `.modal-dialog` class as illustrated here:

```
<div class="modal-dialog modal-lg">
<div class="modal-dialog modal-sm">
```

By default, modals have a fade-in transition effect when shown on a page. This is accomplished by adding the `.fade` class name to the `<div>` element with the `.modal` class name. Here is an example:

```
<div class="modal fade" role="dialog" >
```

If you would like to show the modal instead of fading into the page, simply remove the `.fade` class name.

Tabs

Tabs provide an option to split your content into separate pages. This is an ideal component when you have a particularly large form that you want to split up into a logical grouping. For example, when you're editing an employee's record, you might want to split their basic information from their background history, as illustrated in the following screenshot:

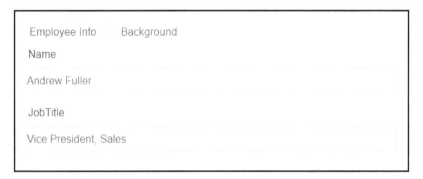

Bootstrap tabs are divided into two parts. You first need to specify the tab names and the ID of the corresponding `<div>` element to show when the user clicks on the tab. This is done by creating a standard unordered list `<ul>` element with the tab names as child list items `<li>`. The `<ul>` element's class must be set to `nav nav-tabs` or `nav nav-pills`, as illustrated in the following HTML markup:

```
<ul class="nav nav-tabs" role="tablist">
    <li class="nav-item">
        <a class="nav-link active" data-toggle="tab" href="#info"
        role="tab">Employee Info</a>
    </li>
    <li class="nav-item">
        <a class="nav-link" data-toggle="tab" href="#background"
        role="tab">Background</a>
    </li>
</ul>
```

You can use a tab or pill navigation by setting the `<li>` element's `data-toggle` attribute to either `tab` or `pill` and setting the `<ul>` element's class to `nav-pills`. Here's an example:

```
<ul class="nav nav-pills" role="tablist">
```

The result will look like the following screenshot in your browser:

To specify the content for the tabs, create a new `<div>` element and set its class to `.tab-content`. Create a `<div>` element for each tab inside the parent `<div>` element and set each tab's `<div>` element's class to `.tab-pane` as follows:

```
<div class="tab-content">
    <div class="tab-pane active" id="info" role="tabpanel">
        <fieldset class="form-group">
            <label asp-for="Name" class="col-md-2 control-label"></label>
            <input asp-for="Name" class="form-control" />
        </fieldset>
        <fieldset class="form-group">
            <label asp-for="JobTitle" class="col-md-2 control-label"></label>
            <input asp-for="JobTitle" class="form-control" />
        </fieldset>
    </div>
    <div class="tab-pane" id="background" role="tabpanel">
        <textarea asp-for="About" rows="3" class="form-control"></textarea>
    </div>
</div>
```

In the preceding markup, we created two tabs and set the `active` tab to the `info` tab by setting its class to `.active`.

You can also activate a specific page using jQuery. To activate the `background` tab as soon as the page loads, use the following code:

```
$(document).ready(function () {
    $('.nav-tabs a[href="#background"]').tab('show');
});
```

Tooltips

Bootstrap's tooltip plugin is an updated version of Jason Frame's jQuery.tipsy plugin. Tooltips can be used to provide users with additional information labels about specific content on your pages or provide insight into what input is expected in form elements.

Bootstrap 4 uses the third-party tether library for positioning. You have to include the Tether library in order to use tooltips with Bootstrap 4. To install and use the Tether library, complete the following steps:

1. Open the bower.json file, which is located in your project's root folder. If you do not see the file in the Visual Studio Solution Explorer, click on the **Show All Files** button on the Solution Explorer toolbar.

2. In the bower.json file, add the following to the list of dependencies:

   ```
   "tether": "1.1.1"
   ```

3. Visual Studio should begin to download the tether library to the wwwroot\lib\tether folder in your project.

4. Next, to include the Tether library on your site pages, open the project's _Layout.cshtml file, which is located in the Views\Shared folder, and add the following highlighted line before the line where you have included the bootstrap.js script:

   ```
   <script src="~/lib/jquery/dist/jquery.js"></script>
   <script src="~/lib/tether/dist/js/tether.js"></script>
   <script src="~/lib/bootstrap/dist/js/bootstrap.js"></script>
   ```

5. To use a tooltip on any element, add a data-toggle="tooltip" attribute to it. You can specify the placement of the tooltip by setting the data-placement attribute to one of the following values: top, bottom, left, and right.

6. Finally, set the value of the data-original-title attribute to specify what text should be shown inside the tooltip.

7. One caveat of tooltips is that, because of performance concerns, the data- API is opt-in, which means you have to initialize the plugin manually. To do this, add the following JavaScript to your page:

   ```
   $(function () {
       $('[data-toggle="tooltip"]').tooltip();
   })
   ```

8. The preceding code finds all elements whose `data-toggle` attribute is set to `tooltip` and initializes the tooltip plugin for these elements. The result will look similar to the following screenshot in your browser:

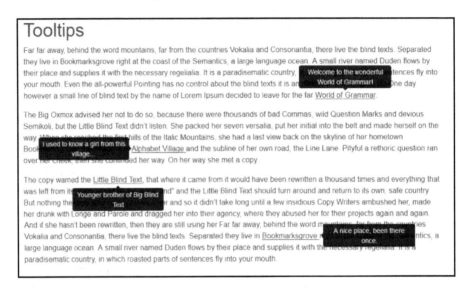

Popovers

Popovers are similar to tooltips in that they can provide users with additional information about an element, but they are designed to show a little more content, as popovers also allow you to display a header.

Popovers are defined in a similar fashion to a popup, by adding the `data-toggle`, `data-placement`, `data-content`, and `title` attributes to an element. The following markup displays a popup when a user clicks on an anchor `<a>` element:

```
<a data-content="The protagonist of Franz Kafka's short story The
Metamorphosis" data-placement="bottom"  data-toggle="popover" href="#"
>Gregor Samsa</a>
```

Setting the `data-toggle` attribute to `popover` specifies to the plugin that it needs to show a popover. The `data-content` attribute contains the content that will be shown inside the popover, and the `data-original-title` attribute sets the title of the popover. The `data-placement` attribute indicates the placement of the popover and supports four values, namely `top`, `bottom`, `left`, and `right`.

You can also specify the trigger that will show the popover by setting the `data-trigger` attribute's value. Popovers can be triggered when a user clicks or hovers over the element, or when the element has focus. You can also specify that the trigger should be activated manually. The four options for the `data-trigger` attribute are `click`, `hover`, `focus`, and `manual`.

As with tooltips, the `data-` API is an opt-in, so you will need to initialize the popover plugin manually. In the following code, using jQuery, we'll find all elements on a page whose `data-toggle` attribute is set to `popover` and initialize the popover plugin for each one:

```
$(function () {
    $('[data-toggle="popover"]').popover();
});
```

The popover plugin will appear similar to the following screenshot in your browser:

The accordion/collapse component

The accordion component is probably best known for FAQ pages or pages that require a lot of content to be broken down into manageable parts. An accordion is made up of a number of panel groups. Each panel group, in turn, has a heading and body elements.

An accordion effect is created by using the Bootstrap collapse plugin which allows you to toggle content in the pages using JavaScript.

To use the accordion component in our project, perform the following steps:

1. To allow the panel to collapse when the user clicks on its heading, we need to add a `data-toggle` attribute to an anchor `<a>` element inside the panel heading element and set its value to collapse.
2. We also need to specify the parent element of the panel by setting the `data-parent` attribute's value to the ID of the parent panel group. Next, set the `anchor` element's `href` attribute to the ID of the `<div>` element that contains the content.
3. Finally, we also need to set the panel body element's class to `.panel-collapse collapse`. In the following code, we'll create an accordion component that contains two panel groups. The first panel group will be automatically visible when the page loads because we'll set its class to `.panel-collapse collapse in`, as follows:

```
<div class="row">
 <div id="accordion" role="tablist" aria-multiselectable="true">
  <div class="panel panel-default">
   <div class="panel-heading" role="tab" id="headingOne">
    <h4 class="panel-title">
     <a data-toggle="collapse" data-parent= "#accordion"
     href="#collapseOne" aria-expanded="true"
     aria-controls="collapseOne">
      How do I order from you?
     </a>
    </h4>
    </div>
    <div id="collapseOne" class="panel-collapse collapse in"
    role="tabpanel" aria-labelledby="headingOne">
     Aliquam erat volutpat. Fusce diam neque, facilisis eu arcu
     eu, vestibulum scelerisque ex. Aenean varius ornare libero at
     rutrum. Nulla dapibus metus vel velit finibus, in tincidunt
eros
     ornare. Sed quis dictum risus. Donec ut orci pulvinar,
tincidunt
     ipsum a, dapibus lectus. Proin dictum feugiat metus nec
```

```
           porttitor. Proin sed diam eget lectus maximus imperdiet ac
           consequat mauris.
             </div>
           </div>
           <div class="panel panel-default">
             <div class="panel-heading" role="tab" id="headingTwo">
               <h4 class="panel-title">
                 <a class="collapsed" data-toggle="collapse"

                   data-parent="#accordion" href="#collapseTwo"
                   aria-expanded="false" aria-controls="collapseTwo">
                    Do you ship internationally?
                 </a>
               </h4>
             </div>
            <div id="collapseTwo" class="panel-collapse collapse"
            role="tabpanel" aria-labelledby="headingTwo">
            Fusce tortor massa, ullamcorper sit amet ligula non, suscipit
            eleifend nisi. Aenean dolor purus, rhoncus a ante nec, tempor
            dapibus ex. Morbi nec pulvinar urna. Maecenas mollis
consectetur
            leo, at ullamcorper elit fermentum vel. Donec arcu neque,
varius
            quis nibh nec, aliquet elementum lacus. Interdum et malesuada
            fames ac ante ipsum primis in faucibus. Vestibulum et rhoncus
            nisl. Mauris egestas posuere elit nec varius.
            </div>
           </div>
         </div>
        </div>
```

The accordion should look similar to the following images, which shows a collapsed accordion and an expanded accordion:

How do I order from you?

Do you ship internationally?

How do I order from you?

Aliquam erat volutpat. Fusce diam neque, facilisis eu arcu eu, vestibulum scelerisque ex. Aenean varius ornare libero at rutrum. Nulla dapibus metus vel velit finibus, in tincidunt eros ornare. Sed quis dictum risus. Donec ut orci pulvinar, tincidunt ipsum a, dapibus lectus. Proin dictum feugiat metus nec porttitor. Proin sed diam eget lectus maximus imperdiet ac consequat mauris.

Do you ship internationally?

The carousel component

The carousel component is a user interface element, which you'll see on a number of websites. It is essentially a slideshow that cycles through different elements, usually images. The carousel component should be contained inside a `<div>` element with a class name of `carousel` and a `data-ride` attribute with a value of `carousel`. To use the carousel component in your project, perform the following steps:

1. The carousel component consists of an ordered list element, `<ol>`, which renders as small circles in the browser and indicates which slide is currently active. The markup for this element is as follows:

```
<ol class="carousel-indicators">
    <li data-target="#carousel" data-slide-to="0"
    class="active"></li>
    <li data-target="#carousel" data-slide-to="1"></li>
    <li data-target="#carousel" data-slide-to="2"></li>
</ol>
```

2. Next, another `<div>` element with a class name of `carousel-inner` needs to be created. This element will contain the actual slides and their content. The following markup creates such an element with one slide:

```
<div class="carousel-inner" role="listbox">
    <div class="carousel-item active">
        <img src="~/img/slide1.jpg" alt="Slide no.1">
    </div>
    <div class="carousel-item">
        <img src="~/img/slide2.jpg" alt="Slide no.2">
    </div>
    <div class="carousel-item">
        <img src="~/img/slide3.jpg" alt="Slide no.3">
    </div>
</div>
```

3. Finally, to add arrows on either side of the carousel to indicate to the user that they can navigate to the next slide, add the following markup to the parent `<div>` element:

```
<a class="left carousel-control" href="#carousel" role="button"
        data-slide="prev">
    <span class="icon-prev" aria-hidden="true"></span>
    <span class="sr-only">Previous</span>
</a>
<a class="right carousel-control" href="#carousel" role="button"
 data-slide="next">
    <span class="icon-next" aria-hidden="true"></span>
    <span class="sr-only">Next</span>
</a>
```

4. The duration for which each slide should be shown can be set via the `data-interval` attribute. In the following markup, we set the interval between slides to 10 seconds:

```
<div id="carousel" class="carousel slide" data-ride="carousel"
data-interval="10000">
```

5. As with all the other plugins, you also have a choice of initializing the plugin and setting its options using JavaScript. In the following code, we'll initialize the carousel and set the interval between slides to 10 seconds:

```
$(function () {
    $('#carousel').carousel({
        interval: 10000
    });
});
```

6. You also have an option to add a caption to each slide in the carousel by adding a `<div>` element with a class name of `.carousel-caption` to the `.carousel-item` element, as illustrated in the following code:

```
<div class="carousel-item">
    <img src="~/img/slide3.jpg" alt="Slide no.3">
        <div class="carousel-caption">
            <h3>A rainy day</h3>
                <p>Rain against a windscreen.</p>
        </div>
</div>
```

Take a look at following screenshot:

Summary

In this chapter, we examined various Bootstrap JavaScript plugins, how to initialize them, and how to set their options using either the `data-` API or the programmatic JavaScript approach.

In the next chapter, we'll explore how you can create your own ASP.NET MVC helpers and Tag helpers to reduce the amount of HTML markup you have to write in order to create a number of Bootstrap elements and components.

5
Creating MVC Bootstrap Helper and Tag Helpers

ASP.NET Core allows developers to create their own HTML Helper methods either by creating static or extension methods. In essence, an HTML Helper is simply a method that returns an HTML string.

HTML Helpers enable you to use the same common block of markup on multiple pages and make the code and markup in your pages easier to read and maintain. This promotes the use of reusable code, and developers can also unit test their helper methods.

ASP.NET Core also introduced a new concept called a **Tag Helper** that serves a similar purpose to a **HTML Helper**. The Tag Helpers is not a replacement for the traditional the HTML Helpers but provides developers with an alternative way to generate cleaner HTML markup.

In this chapter, we will cover the following topics:

- An overview of the built-in ASP.NET Core HTML and Tag Helpers
- Creating HTML Helpers using static methods
- Creating HTML Helper using extension methods
- Creating self-closing helpers
- Creating Tag Helpers

Built-in HTML Helpers

An `HtmlHelper` is a method that renders HTML content inside a view. It is intended to allow developers to reuse a common block of HTML markup across multiple pages.

ASP.NET MVC provides a range of standard, out-of-the-box HTML Helpers. For example, to produce the HTML for a textbox with an ID and name attribute of `CustomerName`, use the following code:

```
<input type="text" name="CustomerName" id="CustomerName">
```

You should use the `TextBox` helper as illustrated:

```
@Html.TextBox("CustomerName")
```

The majority of the built-in HTML Helpers offer several overloaded versions. For instance, to create a textbox and explicitly set its name and value attributes, you should use the following overloaded `TextBox` helper method:

```
@Html.TextBox("CustomerName""","Northwind Traders")
```

Most built-in helpers also offer the option to specify HTML attributes for the element that is generated by passing in an anonymous type. In the following example, we'll create a textbox and set its `style` property using one of the overload methods:

```
@Html.TextBox("CustomerName","Northwind Traders", new { style="background-
color:Blue;" })
```

You can read more about the standard HTML Helpers available in ASP.NET MVC from `http://bit.ly/MVCFormHelpers`.

Built-in Tag Helpers

Tag Helpers are a new feature that have been introduced with ASP.NET MVC Core; their purpose is similar to those of HTML Helpers, but they provide an alternative syntax to the traditional HTML Helpers. Currently, ASP.NET MVC Core provides a range of built-in Tag Helpers; for example, consider the following HTML for a textbox with an ID and a name attribute of `CustomerName`:

```
<input type="text" name="CustomerName" id="CustomerName" class="form-
control">
```

To generate the preceding HTML markup using a Tag Helper and data passed in to the view via a model, you would use the following:

```
<input asp-for="CustomerName" class="form-control" />
```

As you can see, Tag Helpers provide a cleaner syntax and will also make it easier for designers to understand the page markup without having to know any Razor syntax.

 You can learn more about Tag Helpers at `http://bit.ly/TagHelpers`.

The difference between HTML Helpers and Tag Helpers

Tag Helpers are attached to HTML elements inside your Razor views and can help you write markup that is both cleaner and easier to read than the traditional HTML Helpers. HTML Helpers, on the other hand, are invoked as methods that are mixed with HTML inside your Razor views.

Visual Studio also provides minimum IntelliSense support when writing HTML Helpers, as the parameters for the HTML Helper methods are all strings. For example, in the following code, the `LabelFor` and `TextBoxFor` HTML Helper methods are used to create a label and textbox for a model property:

```
<div class="form-group">
    @Html.LabelFor(m => m.Email, new { @class = "col-md-2 control-label" })
    <div class="col-md-10">
        @Html.TextBoxFor(m => m.Email, new { @class = "form-control" })
    </div>
</div>
```

Because the class is a reserved word in C#, you will notice in the preceding code how you have to append the @ sign in order to specify a CSS class name for the label and textbox. For a frontend designer who is familiar with HTML, CSS, and JavaScript, but not C# or Razor, the code would be very hard to read and interpret.

On the other hand, Visual Studio's IntelliSense writes all of the markup for Tag Helpers. For example, the same code shown previously can be written in the following manner using Tag Helpers:

```
<div class="form-group">
    <label asp-for="Email" class="col-md-2 control-label"></label>
    <div class="col-md-10">
        <input asp-for="Email" class="form-control" />
    </div>
</div>
```

The preceding markup can easily be read by a frontend designer, as it uses a standard HTML element, but the elements contain `asp-` attributes. Even though the `asp-` attributes still use strings for their value, Visual Studio, using IntelliSense, assists in writing all of the markup for the Tag Helper.

Creating HTML Helpers using static methods

The simplest way to create a helper in ASP.NET MVC used to be the `@helper` directive. Unfortunately, the `@helper` directive was removed from the new ASP.NET MVC Core, since it imposed too many restrictions on the other Razor features.

Fortunately, we're still able to create an HTML Helper using static method by completing the following steps:

1. Create a new folder called `Helpers` inside the root folder of your project.
2. Add a new class to this folder called `Enums.cs`. This file will contain all the enumerators for our project.
3. Add the following code to the `Enums.cs` file:

```
public class Enums
{
    public enum ButtonStyle
    {
        Default,
        Primary,
        Secondary,
        Success,
        Info,
        Warning,
        Danger
    }
```

```
public enum ButtonSize
{
    Large,
    Small,
    ExtraSmall,
    Normal
}
}
```

4. Create a new static class called `ButtonHelper.cs` in the `Helpers` folder.

5. Add a method called `Button` to the `ButtonHelper` class, and add the following code to it:

```
public static HtmlString Button(string caption, Enums.ButtonStyle
style, Enums.ButtonSize size)
{
    if (size != Enums.ButtonSize.Normal)
    {
        return new HtmlString(
            $"<button type="button" class=
          "btn btn-{style.ToString().ToLower()}
           btn-{ToBootstrapSize(size)}">{caption}</button>");
    }
    return new HtmlString(
        $"<button type="button" class="btn
        btn-{style.ToString().ToLower()}">{caption}</button>");
}
```

6. Finally, add another method called `ToBootstrapSize`:

```
private static string ToBootstrapSize(Enums.ButtonSize size)
{
    string bootstrapSize = string.Empty;
    switch (size)
    {
        case Enums.ButtonSize.Large:
            bootstrapSize = "lg";
            break;

        case Enums.ButtonSize.Small:
            bootstrapSize = "sm";
            break;

        case Enums.ButtonSize.ExtraSmall:
            bootstrapSize = "xs";
            break;
    }
```

```
        return bootstrapSize;
    }
```

The `Button` method we created earlier accepts three parameters in order to set the button's caption, size, and style. We used the enumerator values declared in the `Enums.cs` file in order to list the available sizes and styles for the button, this releases the developer from memorizing the exact Bootstrap class names for each.

The `Button` method returns an `HtmlString` object that represents an HTML-encoded string, which does not need to be encoded again. If we simply return a normal string object, the actual HTML would be rendered inside the view instead of the button.

The `ToBootstrapSize` method basically converts the `ButtonSize` value to a valid Bootstrap class name that represents the size of the button.

Using the static method helper in a view

In order to use the static method helper we created earlier, open the view you intend to use it in, and add the following Razor markup to it:

```
<div class="row">
    @ButtonHelper.Button("Large Danger Button", Enums.ButtonStyle.Danger,
Enums.ButtonSize.Large)
</div>
<div class="row">
    @ButtonHelper.Button("Normal Info Button", Enums.ButtonStyle.Info,
Enums.ButtonSize.Normal)
</div>
<div class="row">
    @ButtonHelper.Button("Small Secondary Button",
Enums.ButtonStyle.Secondary, Enums.ButtonSize.Small)
</div>
```

The result will look similar to the following screenshot:

Creating helpers using extension methods

If we want our helpers to behave in a manner similar to the built-in ASP.NET MVC HTML Helpers, we need to create an extension method. Extension methods are a technique used to add new methods to an existing class.

 Extension methods are a very powerful and intuitive approach to add additional functionality to existing classes and can help you in many ways. You can read more about extension methods on MSDN at http://bit.ly/ExtMethods.

We'll create an extension method to the HtmlHelper class that is represented by a view's HTML property by completing the following steps:

1. Start by adding a new class file called ButtonExtensions.cs to the Helpers folder in the root of your project.
2. Change the class type to static. Extension methods need to be declared inside a static class.
3. Add a new method called BootstrapButton to the class. The first parameter of the method indicates which class the extension extends and must be preceded with the this keyword.
4. The remaining parameters will be used to specify the caption, style, and size of the button. The code for the method is as follows:

```
public static IHtmlContent BootstrapButton(this IHtmlHelper helper,
string caption, Enums.ButtonStyle style, Enums.ButtonSize size)
{
    if (size != Enums.ButtonSize.Normal)
    {
        return new HtmlString(string.Format("<button type="button"
        class="btn btn-{0} btn-{1}">{2}</button>",
        style.ToString().ToLower(), ToBootstrapSize(size),
        caption));
    }
    return new HtmlString(string.Format("<button type="button"
    class="btn btn-{0}">{1}</button>", style.ToString().ToLower(),
    caption));
}
```

The BootstrapButton method is the same as the Button method in the ButtonHelper class we created earlier, apart from the fact that it is an extension to the IHtmlHelper interface.

Using the extension method helper in a view

As the `BootstrapButton` method is an extension method, using it involves opening the view and adding the following markup to it:

```
@using Chapter5.Helpers
<div class="row">
    @Html.BootstrapButton("My Button", Enums.ButtonStyle.Info,
Enums.ButtonSize.Normal)
</div>
```

Note that we're using the standard HTML Helper to invoke the `BootstrapButton` method.

Creating self-closing helpers

Self-closing helpers are helpers that can contain HTML and Razor markup. The built-in `@Html.BeginForm()` helper is an example of this helper type.

In order to create this type of HTML Helper, we'll need to create a helper class that implements the `IDisposable` interface. Using the `IDisposable` interface, we can write the element's closing tags when the object is disposed.

The Bootstrap `Alert` component is a good candidate for such a helper. To create the helper, we'll have to complete the following steps:

1. Create a new subfolder called `Alerts` inside the `Helpers` folder in your project.
2. Open the `Enums.cs` file and add a new item called `AlertStyle`:

   ```
   public enum AlertStyle
   {
       Default,
       Primary,
       Success,
       Info,
       Warning,
       Danger
   }
   ```

3. Add a new class file called `Alert.cs` to the `Alerts` folder.

4. Add a new private, read-only `TextWriter` object field to the class called `_writer`:

```
private readonly TextWriter _writer;
```

5. Create a constructor for the `Alert` class that accepts three parameters. The first is a reference to the `IHtmlHelper` interface, the second specifies the title of the alert, and the third indicates the style of the alert.

6. Add the following code to the `Alert` class's constructor method:

```
public Alert(IHtmlHelper helper, string title,
Enums.AlertStyle style = Enums.AlertStyle.Success)
{
    _writer = helper.ViewContext.Writer;
    var alertDiv = new TagBuilder("div");
    alertDiv.AddCssClass("alert");
    alertDiv.AddCssClass("alert-" + style.ToString().ToLower());
    alertDiv.Attributes.Add("role", "alert");
    alertDiv.TagRenderMode = TagRenderMode.StartTag;
    var strong = new TagBuilder("strong");
    strong.InnerHtml.Append(title);
    string html = ToString(alertDiv) + ToString(strong);
    _writer.Write(html);
}
```

In this code, we've set the `_writer` field to the `Writer` property of the `IHtmlHelper` interface's `ViewContext` property. By utilizing this property, we'll be able to write HTML to the current view.

We then built up the `alert` element's HTML markup using the `TagBuilder` object, and finally, sent the result to the `_writer` object to output. Note that we used a method called the `ToString` method in order to output the `TagBuilder` to a string. The code for the `ToString` method is as follows:

```
public static string ToString(Microsoft.AspNetCore.Html.IHtmlContent
content)
{
    var writer = new System.IO.StringWriter();
    content.WriteTo(writer, System.Text.Encodings.Web.HtmlEncoder.Default);
    return writer.ToString();
}
```

The `<div>` element with the class name `alert` will be closed in the `Alert` class's `Dispose` method, which is implemented in the following manner:

```
public void Dispose()
{
    _writer.Write("</div>");
}
```

Next, add a new file called `AlertHelper.cs` to the `Helpers\Alerts` folder.

```
Add the following code to the AlertHelper class:
public static class AlertHelper
{
    public static Alert Alert(this IHtmlHelper html, string title,
Enums.AlertStyle style = Enums.AlertStyle.Success)
    {
        return new Alert(html, title, style);
    }
}
```

Using the self-closing helper in a view

To use the helper we created earlier in our view, we'll use the C# `using` keyword. The `using` keyword restricts the scope of an object and works well with the `IDisposable` interface. In essence, as soon as the helper has finished rendering its HTML output, the `Dispose` method will automatically be invoked, thus closing the last `<div>` element tag.

To use the helper in a view, use the following markup:

```
@using Chapter5.Helpers.Alerts
<div class="row">
    @using (Html.Alert("Title", Enums.AlertStyle.Success))
    {
        <p>Hello World</p>
        <p>Lorem ipsum dolor sit amet, consectetur adipiscing elit.</p>
    }
</div>
```

The helper will generate the required HTML in order to show the following panel in the browser:

> **Title**
> Hello World
>
> Lorem ipsum dolor sit amet, consectetur adipiscing elit.

Creating a Bootstrap button Tag Helper

Tag Helpers are a new addition to ASP.NET MVC Core and can be used to generate HTML markup. The syntax of Tag Helpers is similar to traditional HTML elements, but is still processed on the server.

Although traditional HTML Helpers are still available, Tag Helpers are intended as an alternative, if not replacement, syntax.

To create your own custom Tag Helper that will generate a Bootstrap button, complete the following steps:

1. Add a new folder called `TagHelpers` to your project.
2. Create a new class called `BootstrapButtonTagHelper` in the `TagHelpers` folder.
3. Change the `BootstrapButtonTagHelper` to inherit from the `TagHelper` class, which is a built-in class of the `Microsoft.AspNetCore.Razor.TagHelpers` package.
4. In order to use the `TagHelper` class, add the following to the top of the `BootstrapButtonTagHelper` class:

   ```
   using Microsoft.AspNetCore.Razor.TagHelpers;
   ```

5. Next, add two properties, called `Color` and `Style`, to the class. The two properties' data types will be set to two enums called `BootstrapColor` and `BootstrapStyle`.

   ```
   public string Color { get; set; }
   public string Size { get; set; }
   ```

6. Lastly, override the `Process` method of the `TagHelper` class and change its code to the following:

```
public override void Process(TagHelperContext context,
TagHelperOutput output)
{
    output.TagName = "button";
    output.Attributes.Clear();
    output.Attributes.Add("class", "btn btn-" + Color + " btn-"
     + Size);
}
```

The code for the `Process` method will set the `output` object's `TagName` property to `button` and add the necessary Bootstrap button classes, based on the values set in the `Color` and `Size` properties, to the generated `<button>` element.

You'll notice that the `Add` method in the `Attributes` collection is used in order to add the class names to the element.

A very good example of custom MVC Tag Helpers, which contains a wealth of code samples (if a little outdated), was created by Daniel Kuon and is available on GitHub at `https://github.com/daniel-kuon/TagHel perExtensions`.

Using the Bootstrap button Tag Helper

Once you've completed the steps to create a Tag Helper, you can use it in your views by following these steps:

1. In order to use the Tag Helper in all your views, you need to open the _ViewImports.cshtml file inside the `Views` folder. If the `Views` folder does not contain a _ViewImports.cshtml file, create a new one.
2. Add the following to the _ViewImports.cshtml file:

```
@addTagHelper "*, Microsoft.AspNetCore.Mvc.TagHelpers"
@addTagHelper "*, Chapter5"
```

The `@addTagHelper` directive enables all views to use Tag Helpers. The first line of the preceding code will add all the built-in ASP.NET MVC Tag Helpers; the second will include all Tag Helpers declared in the `Chapter5` project. The _ViewImports.cshtml is inherited by default by all files, which will enable the Tag Helpers declared in the file for all views by default.

To use the Tag Helper inside your view, open a view and add the following to it:

```
<bootstrap-button color=" danger" size="sm">My Button</bootstrap-button>
```

By specifying the color and size attributes, the preceding statement will generate a small, red Bootstrap button. Tag Helpers work by convention, using what the ASP.NET team calls Kebab case. For example, our helper is called `BootstrapButtonTagHelper`, which means, to use it in your view, you simply have to remove the `Tag Helper` part of the file and add a minus sign between each capital letter, for example, `bootstrap-button`.

The same rule applies for the properties declared inside the Tag Helper, and you'll also notice that each property is an attribute you can set inside the view.

Creating a Bootstrap Alert Tag Helper

To create a Bootstrap Alert Tag Helper, which will be a little bit more advanced than the previous example, follow these steps:

1. Create a new class called `BootstrapAlertTagHelper` in the `TagHelpers` folder.
2. Change the class to inherit from `TagHelper`.
3. Add a Boolean property called `Dismissable` and a `string` property called `Color` to the class:

   ```
   public bool Dismissable { get; set; }
   public string Color { get; set; }
   ```

4. Next, override the `ProcessAsync` method, as illustrated here:

   ```
   public override async Task ProcessAsync(TagHelperContext context,
   TagHelperOutput output)
   {
       output.TagName = "div";
       output.Attributes.Add("class","alert alert-" + Color);
       output.Attributes.Add("role", "attribute");
       if (Dismissable)
           output.PostContent.SetHtmlContent(
       $"<button type="button" class="close" data-dismiss="alert">
       <span aria-hidden="true">&times;</span></button>");

       var content = await output.GetChildContentAsync(true);
   }
   ```

The preceding code will create a new `<div>` element and set its class to `alert` and `alert-*`, depending on the value set in the `Color` property. It will check whether the `Dismissable` property is set to `true`, and, if it is, call a `<button>` element to the end of the content using the `PostContent.SetHtmlContent` method.

Using the Bootstrap Alert Tag Helper

To use the Bootstrap Alert Tag Helper inside your view, use the following:

```
<div class="row">
    <bootstrap-alert color=" danger" dismissable="true">
        <strong>An error occurred</strong> Dismiss me to continue.
    </bootstrap-alert>
</div>
```

The preceding helper code will generate a `red/danger` Bootstrap alert that is also dismissible. Any HTML content specified inside the helper will be rendered inside the Bootstrap Alert.

Summary

In this chapter, you explored how you can decrease the amount of markup in your views using HTML Helpers and Tag Helpers. You also learned how to write helpers that will enable developers who are not familiar with the Bootstrap framework to use helpers to add styled components to their views.

In the next chapter, you'll dive into generating scaffolded views that are correctly styled using the Bootstrap 4 styles and layouts.

6

Converting a Bootstrap HTML Template into a Usable ASP.NET MVC Project

One of the major benefits of using Bootstrap is the wide variety of resources available on the Internet. The web development community has embraced Bootstrap, and you'll find tons of valuable templates, snippets, and advice on using Bootstrap online.

By combining a predesigned Bootstrap template and ASP.NET MVC, you can save a lot of time without having to worry about site layout or design.

In this chapter, we will cover the following topics:

- Why we use prebuilt HTML templates and how they will save time
- Building the master layout
- Adding specific page views
- Including charts in your views

Working with prebuilt HTML templates

It is a well-known fact that most developers are not necessarily good designers. We prefer to work on the backend, building great performing and intelligent software, and sometimes, we tend to think of the user interface as an afterthought.

By using a predesigned HTML Bootstrap template, we can give our users an intuitive and well-designed user interface that was designed by a professional designer. If the design was based on Bootstrap, the developer is already familiar with most of the CSS class names, components, and plugins, and does not have to relearn anything.

The Web offers an assortment of free and premium Bootstrap templates. Themeforest (www.themeforest.net) provides a mind-boggling array of different premium site styles and designs.

With Bootstrap 4, the Bootstrap team also offers official themes, which you can purchase. Each theme provides a full set of tools and examples and can be used as a good starting point for your project.

 The Bootstrap themes can be used to build dashboard, marketing pages, and a variety of web apps. They are competitively priced and are available from http://themes.getbootstrap.com.

For our example in this chapter, we'll use the free Bootstrap 4 Admin Dashboard template available from Bootstrap Zero (www.bootstrapzero.com/bootstrap-template/bootstrap-4-admin-dashboard). The Bootstrap 4 Admin Dashboard template is a basic admin theme that uses Bootstrap 4 and is ideal for a backend administration or a more complex style web application. The theme looks like the following screenshot:

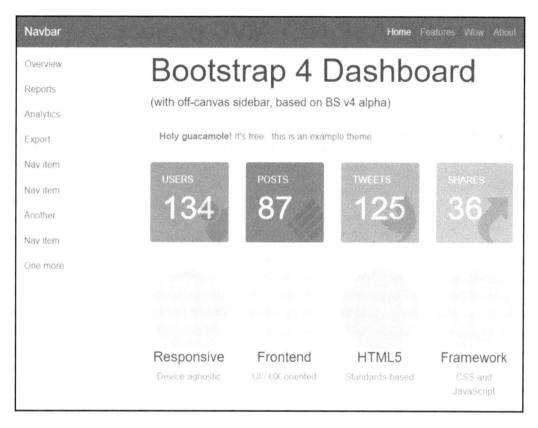

Before we can build an ASP.NET MVC site with the template, we need to download the source files by completing the following steps:

1. Navigate to `http://www.bootstrapzero.com/bootstrap-template/bootstrap-4-admin-dashboard` and click on the **Download** button to download a zip archive containing all the necessary HTML, CSS, and JavaScript files.

2. Extract the files to a folder on your local hard drive; you'll notice that the archive contains the following folders :
   - `css`
   - `js`

3. The archive also contains an `index.html` HTML file that illustrates various page and component layouts of the template, which you'll use as the starting point for designing your project layout.

Creating the ASP.NET MVC project

To create a new ASP.NET MVC project, perform the following steps:

1. In Visual Studio, create a new **ASP.NET Core Web Application** project, as shown in the following screenshot:

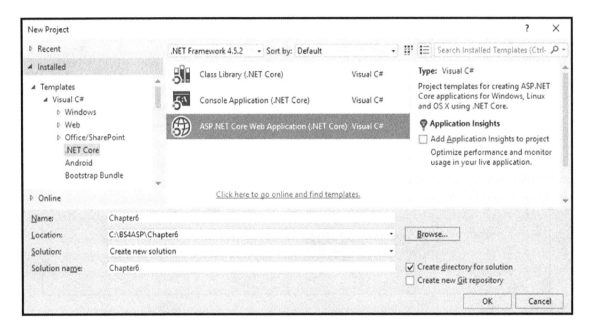

2. In the **New ASP.NET Core Web Application** dialog, select the **Empty** template under the **ASP.NET Core Templates** and click on the **OK** button:

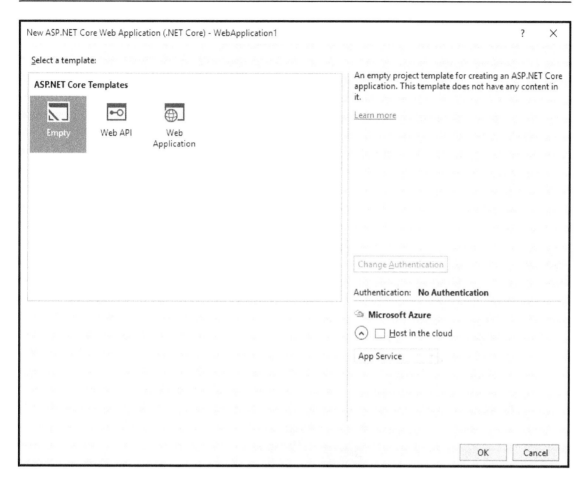

3. Visual Studio will create a default empty MVC project. Right-click on the wwwroot folder inside the project and navigate to **Add | New Folder**. Create the following two folders:
   - css
   - js

4. Add the styles.css file from the Bootstrap 4 Admin Dashboard template css folder to the css folder inside the wwwroot folder in the project.

5. Copy the scripts.js file located in the Bootstrap 4 Admin Dashboard template's js folder to the js folder in the project's wwwroot folder.

6. Next, add two folders to the root of the project called Controllers and Views.

7. Next, in order to enable MVC features such as tooling and Tag Helpers, open the `project.json` file and add the following to the list of dependencies and tools:

```
"dependencies": {
 "Microsoft.NETCore.App": {
 "version": "1.0.0",
 "type": "platform"
 },
 "Microsoft.AspNetCore.Diagnostics": "1.0.0",
 "Microsoft.AspNetCore.Server.IISIntegration": "1.0.0",
 "Microsoft.AspNetCore.Server.Kestrel": "1.0.0",
 "Microsoft.Extensions.Logging.Console": "1.0.0",
 "Microsoft.AspNetCore.Mvc": "1.0.0",
 "Microsoft.AspNetCore.StaticFiles": "1.0.0",
 "Microsoft.AspNetCore.Mvc.TagHelpers": "1.0.0",
 "Microsoft.AspNetCore.Razor.Tools": {
 "version": "1.0.0-preview2-final",
 "type": "build"
 },
 "Microsoft.VisualStudio.Web.CodeGeneration.Tools": {
 "version": "1.0.0-preview2-final",
 "type": "build"
 },
 "Microsoft.VisualStudio.Web.CodeGenerators.Mvc": {
 "version": "1.0.0-preview2-final",
 "type": "build"
 }
 },
"tools": {
 "Microsoft.AspNetCore.Server.IISIntegration.Tools":
 "1.0.0-preview2-final",
 "Microsoft.VisualStudio.Web.CodeGeneration.Tools": {
 "version": "1.0.0-preview2-final",
 "imports": [
 "portable-net45+win8"
 ]
}}
```

8. When you save the `project.json` files, Visual Studio will automatically add all the required dependencies to the project.

9. Open the `Startup.cs` file in the project root and change the `ConfigureService` method to enable MVC, as illustrated here:

```
public void ConfigureServices(IServiceCollection services)
{
    services.AddMvc();
}
```

10. Enable static files and specify a default route by altering the `Configure` method, as shown in the following code:

```
public void Configure(IApplicationBuilder app)
{
    app.UseIISPlatformHandler();
    app.UseStaticFiles();
    app.UseMvc(routes =>
    {
        routes.MapRoute(
            name: "default",
            template: "{controller=Home}/{action=Index}/{id?}");
    });
}
```

Creating the master layout

You've added the CSS and JavaScript files needed to create the master layout file for your project. Next, you need to create a home controller as well as a master layout file. To do this, complete the following steps:

1. Add a new empty controller called `HomeController` to the `Controllers` folder by right-clicking on it and selecting **Add | New Item...**.
2. Select **MVC Controllers Class** from the list of project items and click on the **Add** button.
3. Next, right-click on the `Views` folder in your project and navigate to **Add | New Folder**. Name the folder `Shared`.
4. Right-click on the newly created `Shared` folder and navigate to **Add | New Item...**
5. Select **MVC View Layout Page** in the list of project items and keep the name of the file as `_Layout.cshtml` and click on **Add**.
6. Open the `index.html` file in the Bootstrap 4 Admin Dashboard template source files and copy its contents to the `_Layout.cshtml` file.
7. Change the `<head>` tag to reference the `styles.css` folder in the correct folder, as illustrated in the following code:

```
<head>
    <meta charset="utf-8">
    <title>Bootstrap 4 Dashboard</title>
    <meta name="description" content="A admin dashboard theme that
will
```

```
                            get you started with Bootstrap 4." />
                    <meta name="viewport" content="width=device-width,
                        initial-scale=1.0">

                    <link rel="stylesheet"
            href="//maxcdn.bootstrapcdn.com/bootstrap
                        /4.0.0-alpha/css/bootstrap.min.css" />
                    <link href="//maxcdn.bootstrapcdn.com/font-awesome/4.3.0/css/
                        font-awesome.min.css" rel="stylesheet" />
                    <link rel="stylesheet" href="~/css/styles.css" />
                </head>
```

8. Update the following code just above the closing </body> tag:

```
<script src="//ajax.googleapis.com/ajax/libs/jquery/1.9.1
/jquery.min.js"></script>
<script src="//maxcdn.bootstrapcdn.com/bootstrap/4.0.0-alpha/js

/bootstrap.min.js"></script>
<script src="~/js/scripts.js"></script>
```

9. Next, you'll notice that the page is divided into distinguishable elements:
    - A <nav> class that contains the site's navigation menu
    - A <div> with an ID of main
    - * A <div> with a class name of .col-md-9 col-lg-10 main

10. Leave the <nav> and <div> tags with an ID of main as is, and replace all markup inside the <div class="col-md-9 col-lg-10 main"> element with the @RenderBody() method.

11. Next, add a new file called _ViewStart.cshtml to the root of the Views folder. In order to enable all views to use the new layout file, change its contents to this:

```
@{
 Layout = "_Layout";
 }
```

11. The master layout is now complete; next, you'll need to add a view for the Index action in the home controller.

Adding a view for the home controller

You need to create a view for the home controller's `Index` action in order to test the template. Complete the following steps to accomplish this:

1. Open the `HomeController.cs` file and, if the `HomeController` class does not already contain an Index action method, add it as shown here:

   ```
   public IActionResult Index()
   {
       return View();
   }
   ```

2. Next, right-click on the `Views\Home` folder and **Add** | **New Item...** from the context menu.

3. Select **MVC View Page** from the list of project items, make sure the name is `Index.cshtml`, and click on **Add**:

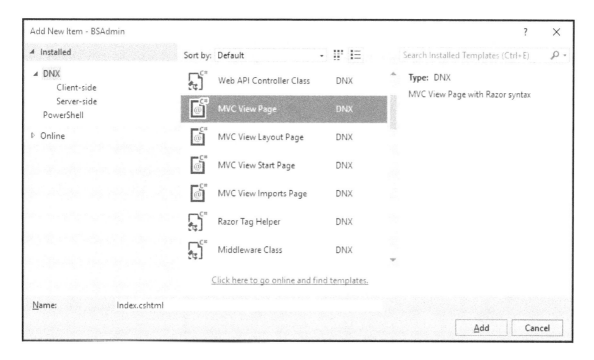

4. Open the newly created Index.cshtml file and change its markup to the following:

```
<p class="hidden-md-up">
    <button type="button" class="btn btn-primary-outline btn-sm"
     data-toggle="offcanvas"><i class="fa fa-chevron-left"></i>

Menu</button>
</p>
<h1 class="display-1 hidden-xs-down">
    Bootstrap 4 Dashboard
</h1>
<p class="lead">(with off-canvas sidebar, based on BS v4 alpha)</p>
<div class="row">
    <div class="col-md-3 col-sm-6">
        <div class="card card-inverse card-success">
            <div class="card-block bg-success">
                <div class="rotate">
                    <i class="fa fa-user fa-5x"></i>
                </div>
                <h6 class="text-uppercase">Users</h6>
                <h1 class="display-1">134</h1>
            </div>
        </div>
    </div>
    <div class="col-md-3 col-sm-6">
        <div class="card card-inverse card-danger">
            <div class="card-block bg-danger">
                <div class="rotate">
                    <i class="fa fa-list fa-4x"></i>
                </div>
                <h6 class="text-uppercase">Posts</h6>
                <h1 class="display-1">87</h1>
            </div>
        </div>
    </div>
    <div class="col-md-3 col-sm-6">
        <div class="card card-inverse card-info">
            <div class="card-block bg-info">
                <div class="rotate">
                    <i class="fa fa-twitter fa-5x"></i>
                </div>
                <h6 class="text-uppercase">Tweets</h6>
                <h1 class="display-1">125</h1>
            </div>
        </div>
    </div>
    <div class="col-md-3 col-sm-6">
```

```
<div class="card card-inverse card-warning">
    <div class="card-block bg-warning">
        <div class="rotate">
            <i class="fa fa-share fa-5x"></i>
        </div>
        <h6 class="text-uppercase">Shares</h6>
        <h1 class="display-1">36</h1>
    </div>
</div>
</div>
</div>
```

5. Run the project, and you should see the home view and layout in your browser:

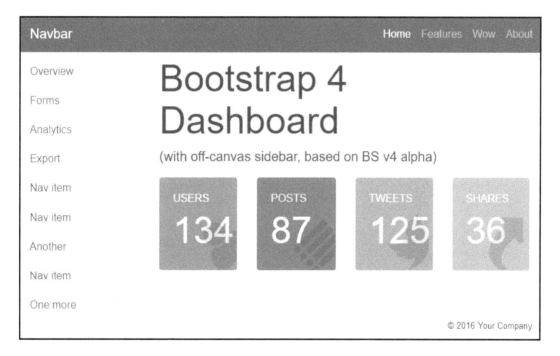

Adding different page views

Next, you'll create a custom view that displays two cards, one with a simple Bootstrap form and another displaying an image, by completing the following steps:

1. Add a new empty **MVC Controller Class** called FormsController.cs to the project's Controllers folder.

2. The new controller class should already contain an `Index` action method.
3. Next, add a new folder called `Forms` inside the `Views` folder.
4. Add a new **MVC View Page**, called `Index.cshtml`, to the newly created `Forms` folder.
5. Add the following markup to the view:

```
<div class="row">
    <h1>Forms</h1>
    <div class="col-md-3">
        <form>
            <div class="card card-success" style="max-width:
20rem;">
                <div class="card-header">
                    First Panel with simple form
                </div>
                <div class="card-block">
                    <fieldset class="form-group">
                        <label for="fullName">Full name</label>
                        <input type="text" class="form-control"
                        id="fullName" placeholder="Your full name">
                    </fieldset>
                    <fieldset class="form-group">
                        <label for="bio">Full name</label>
                        <textarea class="form-control" id="bio"
                          rows="3"></textarea>
                    </fieldset>
                </div>
                <div class="card-footer">
                    <button type="submit" class="btn btn-danger">
                    Save</button>
                </div>
            </div>
        </form>
    </div>
    <div class="col-md-3">
        <div class="card card-primary" style="max-width: 20rem;">
            <div class="card-header">
                Second card
            </div>
            <div class="card-block">
                <img src="http://placehold.it/265x150"/>
            </div>
        </div>
    </div>
</div>
```

6. Finally, you need to change the left-hand side navigation menu to include a link to the view you've just added. To accomplish this, complete the following steps:

7. Open the _Layout.cshtml file inside the Views\Shared folder.

8. Find the following line of code inside the file:

```
<li class="nav-item"><a class="nav-link" href="#">Reports</a></li>
```

9. Replace the preceding line with the following:

```
<li class="nav-item"><a class="nav-link" asp-controller="Forms"

asp-action="Index">Forms</a></li>
```

10. In the preceding code, the asp-* Tag Helpers were used to specify the controller and action for the <a> element. When the user clicks on the **Forms** menu item, they will be shown the form view you created earlier.

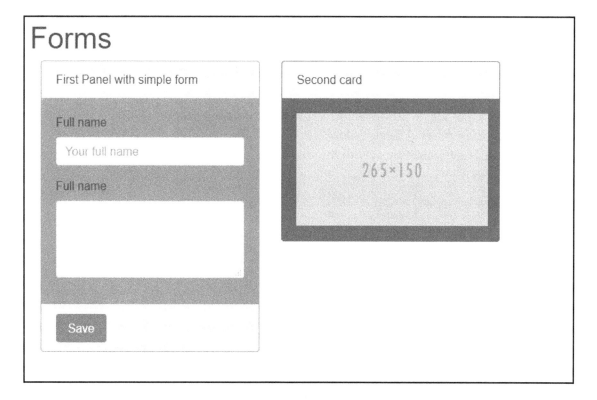

Adding charts to views

By adding charts to your views, you can provide a rich experience for your users and the ability for them to receive an overall view of important information about the system.

There are a number of options when it comes to adding charts and graphs to your project; some of the most popular charting components are as follows:

- Google Charts: `https://developers.google.com/chart/`
- Chart.js: `http://www.chartjs.org/`
- Moris.js: `http://morrisjs.github.io/morris.js/`
- Flot: `http://www.flotcharts.org/`

Adding Google Charts to views

Google provides a rich charting API, which is powerful, easy to use, and free. They also provide an interactive gallery that showcases their many varieties of available charts.

In order to add Google Charts to the Index view of the Home controller, complete the following steps:

1. Inside the Visual Studio Solution Explorer, double-click the `Index.cshtml` file inside the `Views\Home` folder.
2. Add a new Bootstrap row to the view, which will act as the container for the Google chart:

```
<div class="row">
    <div class="col-md-6 col-sm-6" id="piechart">
    </div>
</div>
```

3. Add a reference to the **Google Charts library** as well as a local JavaScript file to the bottom of the page:

```
@section scripts{
    <script type="text/javascript"
src="https://www.gstatic.com/charts        /loader.js"></script>
    <script src="~/js/home.index.js"></script>
}
```

4. Next, add a new JavaScript file called `home.index.js` to the `wwwroot\js` folder.

5. Add the following code to the `home.index.js` file, which will load the Google Charts API as well as specify the call-back function's name to run as soon as the API is loaded:

```
google.charts.load('current', { 'packages': ['corechart'] });
google.charts.setOnLoadCallback(generateChart);
```

6. Next, create the function called `generateChart` inside the file:

```
function generateChart() {
    var data = new google.visualization.DataTable();
    data.addColumn('string', 'Products');
    data.addColumn('number', 'Sales');
    data.addRows([
      ['Tofu', 30],
      ['Chai', 10],
      ['Chocolade', 20],
      ['Ipoh Coffee', 40]
    ]);

    var options = {
        'title': 'Quarterly Sales',
        'width': 600,
        'height': 300,
        is3D: true,
        colors: ['#d9534f', '#f0ad4e', '#5bc0de', '#5cb85c']
    };

    var chart = new
google.visualization.PieChart($('#piechart')[0]);
        chart.draw(data, options);
    }
```

The code in the `generateChart` function creates a new `DataTable` class, which represents a two-dimensional table of values and adds two columns called `Products` and `Sales` to it by calling the `addColumn` method. Four rows of data, containing a product name and total number of products sold, are added to the `DataTable` class, using the `addRows` method.

Next, a new object called options is declared, which contains the options for the Google chart. In these options the colors for the title, size dimensions, and colors for the chart are specified. Setting the `is3D` option to true will generate the chart with a 3D effect.

A new pie chart is declared and its container element, which in this case is a `<div>` element with an `id` of `piechart`, is set. Finally, the chart is drawn by calling the `draw` method.

When running the project, the view should look similar to the following image:

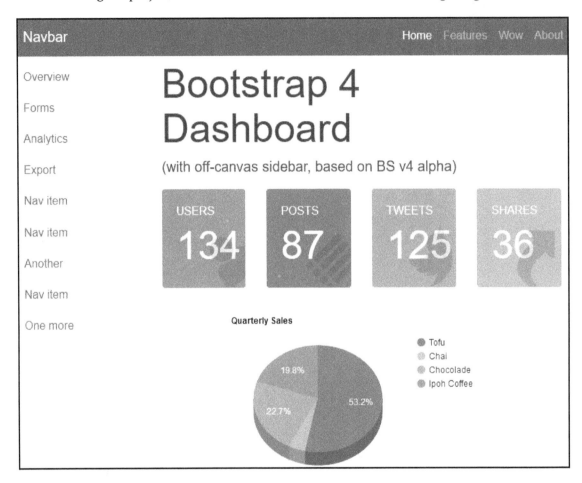

Server-side data processing with Google Charts

In the previous example, the data used for the pie chart was declared inside the JavaScript file. This approach is fine for static data, but in most scenarios you would want to read the data that is used to generate the charts from a data source such as a database.

In order to accomplish this, complete the following steps:

1. Open the `HomeController.cs` file located in the `Controllers` folder.

2. Add a new method called `SalesPerSalesPerson` that will return a JsonResult, as follows:

```
[HttpPost]
public JsonResult SalesPerSalesPerson()
{
    List<object> data = new List<object>();
    data.Add(new string[] { "Product", "Sales" });
    data.Add(new object[] { "Robert King",530});
    data.Add(new object[] { "Nancy Davolio", 1012 });
    data.Add(new object[] { "Laura Callahan", 810 });
    data.Add(new object[] { "Janet Leverling", 738 });
    return Json(data);
}
```

3. In the `SalesPerSalesPerson` method, a new `List` object is declared. The axis names are added as a `string` array, as well as the data for each sales person. This information could also have been read from a database.

4. Next, open the `Index.cshtml` file in the `Views\Home` folder and add the following HTML/Razor mark-up to the file:

```
<div class="col-md-6 col-sm-6" id="barchart"

data-dataurl="@Url.Action("SalesPerSalesPerson","Home")"
</div>
```

5. Note the `<div>` elements' `data-dataurl` attribute will be used in order to pass the URL of the action that will return the data for the chart to the JavaScript function.

6. Open the `home.index.js` file and add the `barChart` JavaScript function:

```
function barChart() {
    var barChart = $('#barchart');
    var dataUrl = barChart.data('dataurl');
    $.post(dataUrl, function (d) {
        var data = google.visualization.arrayToDataTable(d);
        var chart = new google.visualization.BarChart(barChart[0]);

        var options = {
            'title': 'Sales per Representative',
            'width': 600,
            'height': 300
```

```
        };
        chart.draw(data,options);
    });
}
```

7. Next, create a new `generateChart` function that will act as the callback function for the Google Chart API:

```
function generateChart() {
    pieChart();
    barChart();
}
```

8. The pieChart method is the same code used in the previous example.

With the required code in place, you can run your project and the resulting view should contain a pie as well as a bar chart, as displayed in the following image:

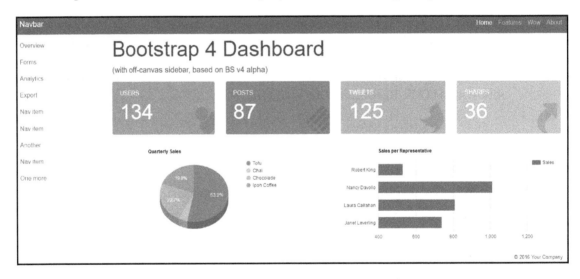

Summary

In this chapter, you've learned how to convert a predesigned HTML template into a usable ASP.NET MVC project. The techniques shown in this chapter can be applied to virtually any HTML template, allowing you to build professionally designed web applications without having to design the layout yourself.

In the next chapter, we'll explore how to include and use the jQuery DataTables plugin in your own ASP.NET MVC projects.

7
Using the jQuery DataTables Plugin with Bootstrap 4

The jQuery`DataTables` plugin allows developers to add innovative interaction controls to any HTML table.

It supports a multitude of options and a wide range of extensions. ASP.NET MVC developers are also able to include this plugin in their own projects. The purpose of this chapter is not only to show you how to use the `DataTables` plugin, but also to illustrate how you can use almost any open source JavaScript and CSS plugin or framework with ASP.NET MVC.

In this chapter, we will cover the following topics:

- An overview of jQuery `DataTables`
- How to include jQuery `DataTables` in your ASP.NET MVC project
- Changing jQuery `DataTables` to support Bootstrap 4
- Loading and displaying data with jQuery `DataTables` and ASP.NET
- Using `DataTables` plugins and extensions

jQuery DataTables

DataTables is a free, open source plugin for the jQuery JavaScript library that was designed and created by a company called SpryMedia Ltd. This plugin makes adding features such as ordering, filtering, pagination, and searching to any standard HTML table incredibly easy to implement.

It also offers various extensions that enable Excel-like features, inline editing, and fixed columns, to name a few. The DataTables website offers well-documented examples, a blog, and a forum, which you can find on www.datatables.net.

The jQuery DataTables plugin can be added to your ASP.NET MVC project in a variety of ways, including NPM, Bower, or the DataTables**Content Delivery Network (CDN)**.

Adding DataTables to your ASP.NET MVC project

To add the basic functionality for the DataTables plugin, the following two files are required:

- The first is jquery.dataTables.css and it contains the default CSS styling for the tables
- The second is jquery.dataTables.js and it contains the JavaScript logic for rendering the DataTables plugin and adding the necessary functionality

Both these files are available at the DataTables CDN at the following links:

- https://cdn.datatables.net/1.1.11/css/jquery.dataTables.min.css

- https://cdn.datatables.net/1.1.11/js/jquery.dataTables.min.js

Using the DataTables Bower package

You can also add all the required CSS and JavaScript files needed for jQuery DataTables as well as all the CSS and JavaScript files for the extensions using Bower. Complete the following steps to add jQuery DataTables when using Bower:

1. In Visual Studio, open the bower.json file. If you do not see the bower.json file inside the Visual Studio Solution Explorer, click on the **Show All Files** button.
2. Add the following two packages to the list of dependencies inside the file:

```
"datatables.net": "1.10.12",
"datatables.net-dt": "1.10.12"
```

3. The `datatables.net` package will add the jQuery DataTables package to the `wwwroot\lib` folder of your project and the `datatables.net-dt` package will add the base styling for jQuery `DataTables`.

4. The `datatables.net` package contains the JavaScript file and the `datatables.net-dt` package will contain the CSS/Stylesheet for `jQuery DataTables`.

Using the CDN

You can either save the files from the aforementioned locations, add them to your project, or rather add a reference to the files hosted on the CDN. The latter option is the preferred approach and will help improve your site's performance.

To reference it from the CDN, complete the following steps:

1. In Visual Studio, open this book's accompanying sample project and open the `_Layout.cshtml` file located inside the `Views\Shared` folder.

2. Inside the `<head>` element of the `_Layout.cshtml` file, add a reference to the jQuery DataTables style sheet by inserting the following line of markup:

```
<link rel="stylesheet" type="text/css" href="//cdn.datatables.net
/1.10.12/css/jquery.dataTables.css">
```

3. Open the view in which you'll need the `DataTables` functionality and add a reference to the JavaScript library by adding the following code to the bottom of the view:

```
@section scripts{
    <script type="text/javascript" language="javascript"
    src="//cdn.datatables.net/1.10.12/js/jquery.dataTables.min.js">
    </script>
}
```

Adding Bootstrap styling to DataTables

The steps mentioned in the preceding section will add the minimum required files to the view and layout file in order to generate the basic styling and functionality for jQuery `DataTables`. However, the default `DataTables` CSS styles can look somewhat out of place in a Bootstrap website.

Luckily, the team behind the DataTables project created a Bootstrap-specific CSS style and JavaScript library to match the look and feel of your site. Both these files are also available on the DataTables CDN:

- https://cdn.datatables.net/1.1.12/css/dataTables.bootstrap4.min.css

- https://cdn.datatables.net/1.1.12/js/dataTables.bootstrap4.min.js

These two files are added in the same way as the normal DataTables CSS and JavaScript files. Bear in mind that when including the Bootstrap-specific DataTables JavaScript file in your view, you need to include a reference to both the default DataTables JavaScript files as well as the Bootstrap-specific file, as illustrated in the following markup:

```
@section scripts{
    <script type="text/javascript" language="javascript"
      src="//cdn.datatables.net/1.10.12/js/jquery.dataTables.min.js">
    </script>
    <script type="text/javascript" language="javascript"
      src="//cdn.datatables.net/1.10.12/js/dataTables.bootstrap4.min.js">
    </script>
}
```

Loading and displaying data in jQuery DataTables

In order to implement the jQueryDataTables plugin, you'll first need to create a new view that will list data inside an HTML table. For this example, you'll create a view that displays a list of customers. The list can be read from any data source, such as a SQL Server database. In this example, a simple List object will be used.

To accomplish this, complete the following steps:

1. In Visual Studio, add a new controller class called CustomerController.cs to the Controllers folder.
2. Add a new folder called Models to the root of your project and add a new class called Customer.cs to it.

3. The `Customer` class will be used to retrieve a list of sample customer records. The code for the class is as follows:

```
public class Customer
{
    public string CustomerCode { get; set; }
    public string CompanyName { get; set; }
    public string ContactName { get; set; }
    public string ContactTitle { get; set; }
    public string Address { get; set; }
    public string City { get; set; }
    public DateTime CreatedDate { get; set; }
}
```

4. Next, open the `CustomerController` class and add a new method called `GetCustomers`. For a complete listing of the `GetCustomers` method, please refer to this chapter's accompanying sample project. This method will simply return a list of sample customer data, as illustrated in the following code:

```
public List<Customer> GetCustomers()
{
    var customers = new List<Models.Customer>
    {
        new Models.Customer() {
            CustomerCode = "ALFKI",
            CompanyName = "Alfreds Futterkiste",
            ContactName = "Maria Anderson",
            ContactTitle = "Sales Representative",
            Address = "Obere Str. 57",
            City = "Berlin",
            CreatedDate = new DateTime(2016,01,12) },
        new Models.Customer() {
            CustomerCode = "AROUT",
            CompanyName = "Around the Horn",
            ContactName = "Thomas Hardy",
            ContactTitle = "Sales Representative",
            Address = "120 Hanover Sq.",
            City = "London",
            CreatedDate = new DateTime(2015,10,14) },
        new Models.Customer() {
            CustomerCode = "CHOPS",
            CompanyName = "Chop-suey Chinese",
            ContactName = "Yang Wang",
            ContactTitle = "Owner",
            Address = "Hauptstr. 29",
            City = "Bern",
            CreatedDate = new DateTime(2010,7,14) },
```

```
new Models.Customer() {
    CustomerCode = "EASTC",
    CompanyName = "Eastern Connection",
    ContactName = "Ann Devon",
    ContactTitle = "Sales Agent",
    Address = "35 King George",
    City = "London",
    CreatedDate = new DateTime(2015,10,15)},
    ...
};
return customers;
}
```

5. In order to retrieve a list of customers and pass the data to the view, change the `Index` method on the `CustomerController` to the following:

```
public IActionResult Index()
{
    var model = GetCustomers();
    return View(model);
}
```

6. Next, create a new sub-folder called `Customer` inside the `Views` folder.
7. Right-click on the newly created `Customer` folder and select **Add | New Item...** from the context menu.
8. Select **MVC View Page** from the list of items, name the file `Index.cshtml`, and click on **Add**, as shown in the following screenshot:

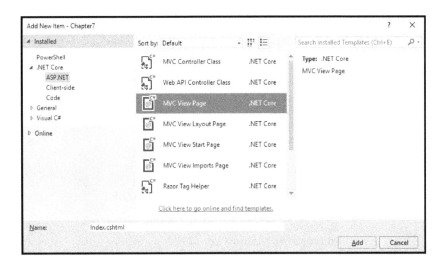

9. Change the markup for the newly added view to the following:

```
@model IEnumerable<Chapter8.Models.Customer>
@{
    Layout = "_Layout";
}
<div class="container">
    <h1>Customer List</h1>
    <div class="row">
        <table id="customer-table"
         class="table table-striped table-bordered">
            <thead>
            <tr>
                <th>Code</th>
                <th>Company Name</th>
                <th>Contact Name</th>
                <th>Address</th>
                <th>City</th>
                <th>Created</th>
            </tr>
            </thead>
            <tbody>
            @foreach (var customer in Model)
            {
                <tr>
                    <td>@customer.CustomerCode</td>
                    <td>@customer.CompanyName</td>
                    <td>@customer.ContactName</td>
                    <td>@customer.Address</td>
                    <td>@customer.City</td>
                    <td>@customer.CreatedDate.ToString("d")</td>
                </tr>
            }
            </tbody>
        </table>
    </div>
</div>
```

In this markup, the `table-striped`, `table-hover`, and `table-bordered` styles have been added to the table whose `id` attribute has been set to `customer-table`. You'll also notice that the column header names have been wrapped inside a `<thead>` element and the table rows inside a `<tbody>` element.

The HTML markup for the view is now ready. Complete the following steps to enable the jQuery DataTable functionality for the table:

1. Open the `_Layout.cshtml` file in the `Views\Shared` folder.

2. Add references to the jQuery `DataTables` base and the Bootstrap style sheets by adding the following mark-up inside the `<head>` element:

```
<link rel="stylesheet" type="text/css" href="~/css/bootstrap.css" />
<link rel="stylesheet" type="text/css" href="//cdn.datatables.net
/1.10.11/css/dataTables.bootstrap4.min.css">
```

3. Scroll to the bottom of the `_Layout.cshtml` file and add a reference to the jQuery as well as the Bootstrap JavaScript files:

```
<script src="~/lib/jquery/dist/jquery.js"></script>
<script src="~/lib/bootstrap/dist/js/bootstrap.js"></script>
```

4. Also, make sure that you have a section declaration for a section called scripts at the bottom of the `_Layout.cshtml` file:

```
@RenderSection("scripts", required: false)
```

5. Open the `Index.cshtml` file in the `Views\Customer` folder. Add the following code to the bottom of the file:

```
@section scripts{
    <script type="text/javascript"
src="//cdn.datatables.net/1.10.11/js/jquery.dataTables.min.js">
    </script>
    <script type="text/javascript"
      src="//cdn.datatables.net/1.10.11
        /js/dataTables.bootstrap4.min.js">
    </script>
    <script type="text/javascript">
        $(document).ready(function () {
            $('#customer-table').DataTable();
        });
    </script>
}
```

In the preceding steps, you've added the required references to the `DataTables` style sheets as well as the JavaScript files. You also created a jQuery event handler, which will enable the DataTable functionality on all HTML elements with a class name of `table` as soon as the page loads.

When you run your project and navigate to the customers view, you'll see that the list of customers are automatically paginated into groups of ten and you are able to search and sort the data inside the table, as shown in the following screenshot. The default Bootstrap 4 styles for tables are also correctly applied:

DataTables plugins

jQuery DataTables provides a lot of built-in features and flexibility, but if you wish to add your own features or need extra flexibility, it does provide a plugin architecture.

These are just some of the plugins available for the DataTables library. To see a full list of available plugins, visit `https://datatables.net/plug-ins/index`

Date sorting

Because of the wide variety of different date formats, sorting dates can sometimes prove to be very challenging. Fortunately, jQuery `DataTables` provides a flexible solution for sorting date fields using the `Moment.js` JavaScript library.

 Moment.js is a free and open source library that makes it easy to display, parse, manipulate, and validate dates in JavaScript. You can read more about the Moment.js library at

`http://momentjs.com/.`

To enable date sorting on the `Created Date` column used in the previous example, complete the following steps:

1. Open the `Index.cshtml` file inside the `Views\Customer` folder.

2. Include the `moment.js` library in your view by adding the following code to the end of the `Index.cshtml` file. Be sure to add it after the `dataTables.bootstrap.min.js` file:

   ```
   <script type="text/javascript"
   src="//cdnjs.cloudflare.com/ajax/libs/moment.js/2.8.4/moment.min.js">
       </script>
   ```

3. Next, add the `DataTables` sorting plugin to the view by adding the following line after the `moment.js` file:

   ```
   <script type="text/javascript" src="//cdn.datatables.net/plug-ins/1.10.11/sorting/datetime-moment.js"></script>
   ```

4. Finally, change the JavaScript code in the view to initialize the moment sorting library. You can specify the date format which should be sorted by passing it as a parameter:

   ```
   <script type="text/javascript">
       $(document).ready(function () {
           $(document).ready(function () {
               $.fn.dataTable.moment('DD/MM/YYYY');
               $('#customer-table').DataTable();
           });
       });
   </script>
   ```

Rendering

jQuery DataTables rendering plugins can be used to change the way data is displayed inside the table. In order to restrict data (in this example, the company name) to a particular length and showing anything longer as an ellipsis (…), for example, Northwind …, complete the following:

1. Open the `Index.cshtml` file inside the `Views\Customer` folder.
2. Add the `DataTables` ellipsis data rendering plugin by including the following at the bottom of the view and after the jQuery `DataTables` library:

```
<script type="text/javascript" src="//cdn.datatables.net/plug-
ins/1.10.11/dataRender/ellipsis.js"></script>
```

3. Change the `DataTables` initialization code to use the Ellipsis plugin. The targets parameter is used to specify which column to use the plugin on:

```
$('#customer-table').DataTable({
    columnDefs: [{
        targets: 1,
        render: $.fn.dataTable.render.ellipsis(15, true)
    }]
});
```

The Ellipsis plugin accepts three parameters; the first is the number of characters to restrict the display to and the second is a boolean value that indicates whether the truncation should not occur in the middle of a word. The last boolean parameter is used to escape HTML entities.

DataTables extensions

The jQuery DataTables plugin provides a wide variety of extensions that can enhance the functionality of the plugin dramatically.

> To see a list of all available extensions for the DatatTables library, see
> `https://datatables.net/extensions/index`

The ColReorder extension

The ColReorder extension allows users to reorder table columns by clicking and dragging the column header to the location they prefer. To enable column reordering for your DataTables HTML table, complete the following steps:

1. Open the `_Layout.cshtml` file and add a reference to the `dataTables.colReorder.css` file:

   ```
   <link rel="stylesheet" type="text/css"
   href="https://cdn.datatables.net
   /colreorder/1.3.1/css/colReorder.bootstrap.min.css" />
   ```

2. Open the view `.cshtml` file and add a reference to the `DataTables colReorder` extension JavaScript file:

   ```
   <script type="text/javascript" charset="utf8"
   src="//cdn.datatables.net
       /colreorder/1.3.1/js/dataTables.colReorder.min.js"></script>
   ```

3. Lastly, using jQuery, add an event handler to initialize the `DataTables` plugin and the colReorder extension after the page has loaded:

   ```
   $('#customer-table').DataTable({
       colReorder: true
   });
   ```

4. When navigating to the page, you should now be able to drag and reorder the columns in the table. A blue line will be displayed when dragging a column, as illustrated in the following screenshot:

Notice that all the style sheets and JavaScript files for the extensions are referenced from the `DataTables` CDN. The CDN is available at `cdn.datatables.net`

The ColVis buttons extension

The ColVis extension adds a button to the top of a DataTable, which, when clicked on, displays a list of column names in the table with a checkbox next to it. The user can then deselect the column names they do not wish to see in the grid.

To enable the column visibility extension, perform the following steps:

1. Open the `_Layout.cshtml` file and add a reference to the Bootstrap 4-specific stylesheet of the `DataTables` buttons extensions:

```
    <link rel="stylesheet" type="text/css"
href="https://cdn.datatables.net
    /buttons/1.1.2/css/buttons.bootstrap4.min.css" />
```

2. Open the `view.cshtml` file and add a reference to the `DataTables` buttons extension, the Bootstrap 4-specific buttons extension, as well as the buttons ColVis extension:

```
    <script type="text/javascript"
src="//cdn.datatables.net/buttons/1.1.2/js/dataTables.buttons.min.js">
    </script>
    <script type="text/javascript"
src="//cdn.datatables.net/buttons/1.1.2/js/buttons.bootstrap4.min.js">
    </script>
    <script type="text/javascript"
src="//cdn.datatables.net/buttons/1.1.2/js/buttons.colVis.min.js">
    </script>
```

3. Lastly, using jQuery, add an event handler to initialize the `DataTables` plugin and the ColVis extension after the page has loaded:

```
    $('#customer-table').DataTable({
        dom: 'Bfrtip',
        buttons: [
            'colvis'
        ]
    });
```

The code in the last step uses the `dom` parameter in order to specify where the control element is placed in the DOM. For buttons, use the letter `B`. When navigating to the view, you should see a button next to the search box with which you can show or hide columns in the table, as shown in the following screenshot:

The copy and print buttons extension

Using the same`DataTables` extension, you can add a toolbar to the table with which the user can copy the data inside the table to the clipboard or present a print view of the data inside the table. It is a really simple way to give your users the ability to export or print their data.

To enable the copy and print functionality for the tables, perform the following steps:

1. Open the `_Layout.cshtml` file and add a reference to the Bootstrap 4-specific stylesheet of the `DataTables` buttons extensions:

```
<link rel="stylesheet" type="text/css"
href="https://cdn.datatables.net
      /buttons/1.1.2/css/buttons.bootstrap4.min.css" />
```

2. Next, open the view and add a reference to the `DataTables` Buttons extension, the Bootstrap 4-specific buttons extension, the HTML 5 buttons extension, as well as the print button extension:

```
<script type="text/javascript"
src="//cdn.datatables.net/buttons/1.1.2/js/dataTables.buttons.min.js">
    </script>
    <script type="text/javascript"
src="//cdn.datatables.net/buttons/1.1.2/js/buttons.bootstrap4.min.js">
    </script>
    <script type="text/javascript"
      src="//cdn.datatables.net/buttons/1.1.2/js/buttons.html5.min.js">
    </script>
    <script type="text/javascript"
      src="//cdn.datatables.net/buttons/1.1.2/js/buttons.print.min.js">
    </script>
```

3. Lastly, using jQuery, add an event handler to initialize the DataTable plugin and add the print and copy buttons to it after the page has loaded:

```
$(document).ready(function () {
    $('#customer-table').DataTable({
        dom: 'Bfrtip',
        buttons: [
            'copy', 'print'
        ]
    });
});
```

When opening the view with the DataTable, you should see two buttons above the DataTable, as shown in the following screenshot:

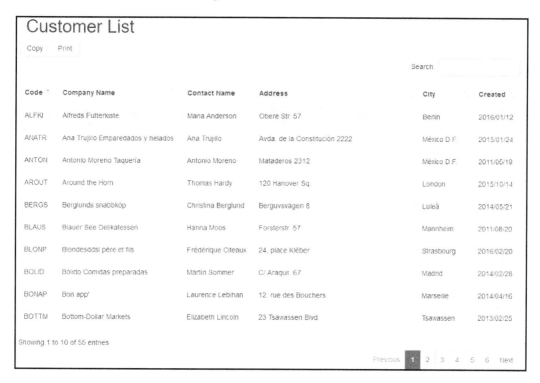

When the user clicks on the **Copy** button, they should see a message informing them that the number of rows in the table has been copied to their clipboard:

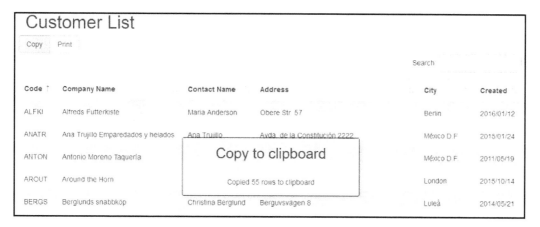

If the user clicks on the **Print** button, a new browser window will open with a printer friendly version of the data inside the DataTable and the print dialog will be displayed:

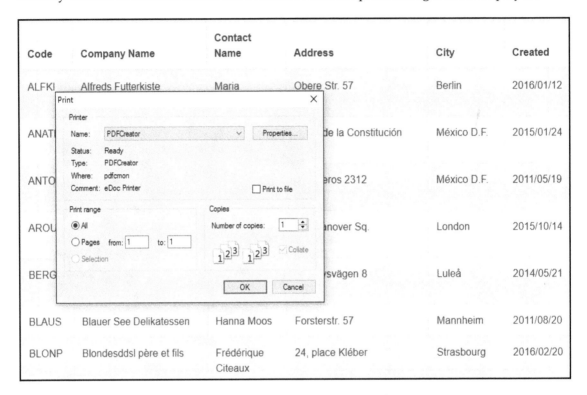

Summary

In this chapter, you've implemented a sortable, searchable, and extendible HTML table using the jQuery `DataTables` plugin. You've also explored how to specify that the plugin should use the Bootstrap 4 styles. This chapter should also have given you the confidence to explore other open source plugins and incorporate them into your own ASP.NET MVC projects.

In the next and last chapter, you'll learn more about using the free Visual Studio Code editor to create ASP.NET MVC sites that use Bootstrap 4 for styling.

8

Creating Bootstrap 4 ASP.NET MVC Sites Using Visual Studio Code

During their Build 2015 conference, Microsoft unveiled a new lightweight code editor for writing web and mobile apps called **Visual Studio Code**. This was a major step for Microsoft, since it marked the first time they offered developers a cross-platform code editor that works on Windows, OS X, and Linux.

With the significant redesign of ASP.NET, which made it an open source and cross-platform framework, developers are now able to create ASP.NET websites on Windows, Linux, and OS X. Visual Studio Code makes this a little bit easier.

In this chapter, we will cover the following topics:

- What is Visual Studio Code?
- Installing Visual Studio Code
- Scaffolding an empty ASP.NET project using Yeoman
- Adding the Bootstrap 4 files using Bower
- Compiling the Bootstrap Sass files using Gulp
- Creating a layout file that references the Bootstrap files

What is Visual Studio Code?

Visual Studio Code, in essence, is an open source, cross-platform text editor. It is based on the **Electron framework**, formerly known as **Atom Shell**, which is a framework that enables you to write cross-platform desktop applications using HTML, CSS, and JavaScript. If you've ever used the Atom text editor by GitHub, you'll see a strong resemblance between that and Visual Studio Code.

 Atom is a hackable/customizable text editor from GitHub. It is also open source and can be downloaded from `https://atom.io/`.

Visual Studio Code can be used by developers to build web applications in HTML, CSS, and JavaScript, and also supports TypeScript and ASP.NET Core. It is folder-based rather than project-based, which means you simply need to open a folder containing your project files instead of opening a project file such as `.csproj`.

It features**IntelliSense** (which will be familiar to anyone that has used Visual Studio in the past) and also supports debugging and Git Source control features. It also includes a few features that Visual Studio developers have come to appreciate, such as syntax highlighting, auto indent, and bracket matching. Visual Studio Code is customizable in the sense that users can change the theme, preferences, and keyboard shortcuts. With the latest release, it also supports extensions, and there are already a wide range of extensions and themes available on `https://marketplace.visualstudio.com/VSCode`.

Installing Visual Studio Code

Installing Visual Studio Code is as simple as downloading the platform installer that is specific to your operating system. You can visit `https://code.visualstudio.com/` and the site should pick up which operating system you're using and display a download button.

For example, since I'm visiting the site from a Windows PC, it automatically displays a **Download for Windows** button:

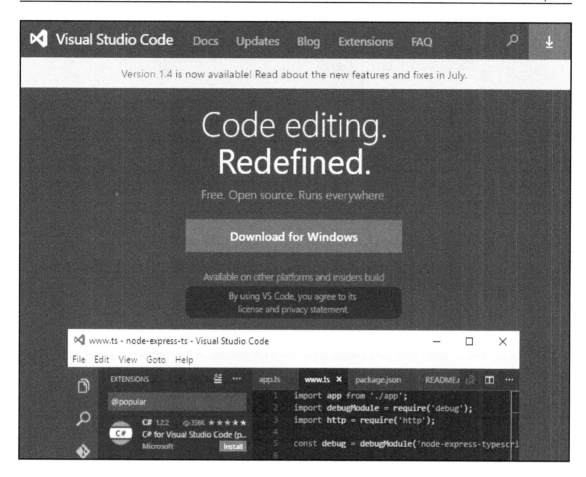

If you need to download it for either Linux or OS X, scroll to the bottom of the page and click on the appropriate download button:

For complete instructions on getting up and running with Visual Studio Code on Mac OS X, Linux, or Windows, visit http://code.visualstudio.com/Docs/editor/setup.

Creating an empty ASP.NET project

Because Visual Studio Code is folder-based and not project-based like Visual Studio, it does not have a **File** | **New Project** option in its list of menus.

Scaffolding a project using Yeoman

Instead, you'll use **Yeoman** to scaffold a basic empty ASP.NET project. If you do not already have npm installed, complete the following steps:

1. Open a new command prompt and navigate to the folder where you would like to create your project, for example, C:\MyBootstrap4Site.

2. Enter the following command in the command prompt in order to install Yeoman and supporting tools:

```
npm install -g yo grunt-cli generator-aspnet bower
```

After Yeoman and supporting tools have been installed, follow these steps:

2. Enter the following command and press *Enter* to start the Yeoman ASP.NET generator:

```
yo aspnet
```

3. Select **Empty Application** from the list of applications and press Enter:

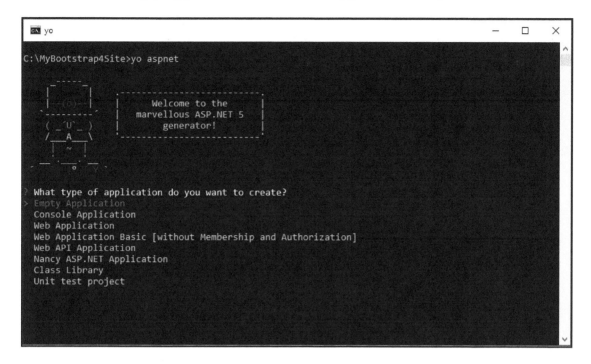

4. When prompted for the name of your ASP.NET application, type `Bootstrap4Site` and press *Enter*.

5. Yeoman will scaffold your project and when finished display a message. Next, restore any packages for your project by entering the following command in the command prompt and press the *Enter* key:

   dnu restore

6. Keep the current command prompt open and start Visual Studio Code.

7. Select **Open Folder...** from the **File** menu inside Visual Studio Code and select the `C:\MyBootstrap4Site` folder.

8. The project folder and files will be displayed inside the Visual Studio Code explorer.

If you receive an error stating that `dnu is not recognized`, run the following command: `dnvm upgrade`.

Enabling ASP.NET MVC and static files

Currently, the project is simply an empty ASP.NET project that will only show a **Hello World** message when run. You'll need to enable your project and MVC to serve static files by completing the following tasks:

1. Open the `project.json` file and change the `dependencies` and tools array to the following:

```
"dependencies": {
    "Microsoft.NETCore.App": {
      "version": "1.0.0",
      "type": "platform"
    },
    "Microsoft.AspNetCore.Diagnostics": "1.0.0",
    "Microsoft.AspNetCore.Mvc": "1.0.0",
    "Microsoft.AspNetCore.Razor.Tools": {
      "version": "1.0.0-preview2-final",
      "type": "build"
    },
    "Microsoft.AspNetCore.Server.IISIntegration": "1.0.0",
    "Microsoft.AspNetCore.Server.Kestrel": "1.0.0",
    "Microsoft.AspNetCore.StaticFiles": "1.0.0",
    "Microsoft.Extensions.Configuration.EnvironmentVariables":
"1.0.0",
    "Microsoft.Extensions.Configuration.Json": "1.0.0",
    "Microsoft.Extensions.Configuration.CommandLine": "1.0.0",
    "Microsoft.Extensions.Logging": "1.0.0",
    "Microsoft.Extensions.Logging.Console": "1.0.0",
    "Microsoft.Extensions.Logging.Debug": "1.0.0",
    "Microsoft.Extensions.Options.ConfigurationExtensions":
"1.0.0",
    "Microsoft.VisualStudio.Web.BrowserLink.Loader": "14.0.0"
  },

  "tools": {
    "BundlerMinifier.Core": "2.0.238",
    "Microsoft.AspNetCore.Razor.Tools": "1.0.0-preview2-final",
    "Microsoft.AspNetCore.Server.IISIntegration.Tools":
      "1.0.0-preview2-final"
  }
```

2. Next, in order to restore the dependencies, switch back to the command prompt and enter the following command followed by the *Enter* key:

    dotnet restore

3. After the dependencies have been restored, switch back to Visual Studio Code and change the `ConfigureServices` method in the `Startup.cs` class file to the following, in order to enable MVC:

```
public void ConfigureServices(IServiceCollection services)
{
    services.AddMvc();
}
```

4. Enable the serving of static files such as images, style sheets, and JavaScript files. Also, set the default route by changing the `Configure` method in the `Startup.cs` class file to the following:

```
public void Configure(IApplicationBuilder app)
{
    app.UseStaticFiles();

    app.UseMvc(routes =>
    {
        routes.MapRoute(
            name: "default",
            template: "{controller=Home}/{action=Index}/{id?}");
    });
}
```

Adding a default route controller and view

Since an empty project was created, no default controller or view would have been created by default. You've already configured a default route in the previous steps and in order for it to work you'll need to add a Home controller and an Index view:

1. Hover over the folder name inside the Visual Studio Code explorer and click on the **New Folder** icon.

2. Name the new folder Controllers and add another folder called Views.

3. Create two more folders called Home and Shared inside the newly created Views folder.

4. Next, right-click on the Controllers folder and select **New File** from the context menu. Name the file HomeController.cs.

5. Add the following code, which will create a default Index method for the controller, to the HomeController.cs file:

```
using Microsoft.AspNetCore.Mvc;
namespace BS4App.Controllers
{
    public class HomeController : Controller
    {
        public IActionResult Index()
        {
            return View();
        }
    }
}
```

6. Add a new file called Index.cshtml to the Views\Home folder and set its content to the following:

```
<h1>This is my Bootstrap 4 site. </h1>
```

7. Your project layout should look similar to the following inside the Visual Studio Code Explorer:

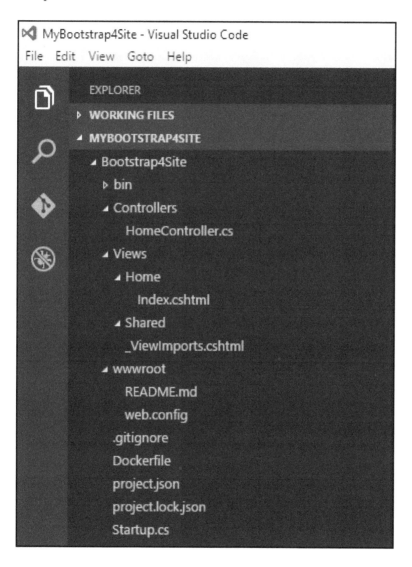

Using Bower to add the Bootstrap 4 files

In order to use Bootstrap 4 in your project, you first need to add the Bootstrap style sheet and JavaScript files. In this example, you'll use Bower to download the Bootstrap 4 files to your local project:

1. Add a new file called `bower.json` to the root of your project folder and set its content to the following in order to add Bootstrap 4 as a dependency:

```
{
  "name": "ASP.NET",
  "private": true,
  "dependencies": {
    "bootstrap": "4.0"
  }
}
```

2. In order to download any Bower dependencies, you'll need to open a new command prompt in your project folder—this can be done from within Visual Studio Code using the keyboard shortcut *Shift + Ctrl + C*.
3. Enter the following command inside the command prompt and press *Enter*:

```
bower update
```

4. The previous command will download any Bower dependencies specified inside the `bower.json` file and save it to a `bower_components` folder inside your project.

5. After the Bower dependencies has been downloaded, your project layout should resemble the following inside the Visual Studio Code explorer:

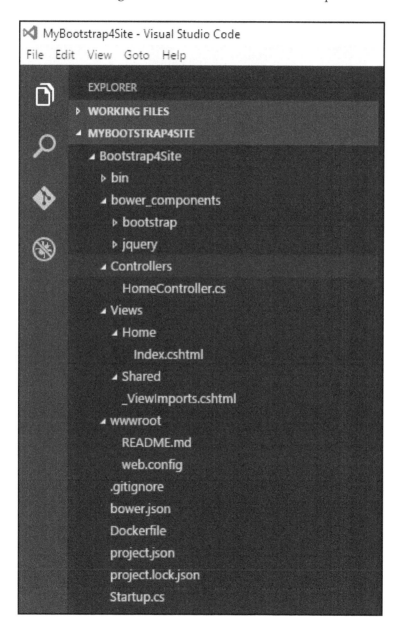

If you receive the following error, `ENOGIT git is not installed or not in the PATH`, it means that you do not have the Git installation folder path specified in your environment variables. Fix this by adding the following values to your Windows environment variables:
`;%PROGRAMFILES(x86)%\Git\bin;%PROGRAMFILES(x86)%\Git\cmd`
Another workaround is to run the command from the Git Shell instead of the normal command prompt.

Using Gulp to compile the Bootstrap Sass files

If you would like the option to customize the Bootstrap Sass files in order to use them in your project, you can automate the Sass compilation process by creating a Gulp task for it.

Visual Studio Code supports the ability to run tasks and analyze their results from inside it. Task can include many things such as compiling Sass, minifying CSS, or copying files to different folders.

In order to configure task inside Visual Studio Code, follow these steps:

1. Inside Visual Studio Code, open the **Command Palette** by pressing the *F1* key.
2. Type the following inside the Command Palette and press *Enter:*

   `Configure Task Runner`

3. Select **Grunt** from the list and press the *Enter* key.
4. The command will automatically create a new folder called `.vscode` with a new `tasks.json` file inside it.
5. You'll need Gulp and the gulp-sass plugin in order to compile the Bootstrap 4 SCSS files to CSS. To install this plugin, open the command prompt and enter the following commands, followed by the *Enter* key:

   `npm install gulp gulp-sass`

6. After the necessary plugins have been installed, switch back to Visual Studio Code and change the contents of the `tasks.json` file to the following:

   ```
   {
       "version": "0.1.0",
       "command": "gulp",
       "isShellCommand": true,
   ```

```
        "tasks": [
            {
                "taskName": "compile-sass",
                "isBuildCommand": true,
                "showOutput": "always",
                "isWatching": true
            }
        ]
    }
```

7. Save the `tasks.json` file and add a new file called `gulpfile.js` to the root of your project.

8. Change the contents of the `gulpfile.js` file to the following:

```
var gulp = require('gulp');
var gulpSass = require('gulp-sass');

gulp.task('compile-sass', function () {
    gulp.src('./bower_components/bootstrap/scss/bootstrap.scss')
        .pipe(gulpSass())
        .pipe(gulp.dest('./wwwroot/css'));
});
```

9. The previous changes will compile the `bootstrap.scss` SASS file located in the `./bower_components/bootstrap/scss/` folder and copy the CSS file to the `wwroot/css` folder as `bootstrap.css`.

10. In order to run the compile-sass task, press the *F1* key to bring up the Command Palette and type the following, or select it from the list of items:

    Tasks: Run Task

11. This will return a list of available tasks configured in your project. Select `compile-sass` from the list.

12. Visual Studio Code will show an output window with the result of the task:

```
OUTPUT                                                    Tasks      ▾  ≝  ✕
  [13:35:36] Using gulpfile c:\VSCodeProjects\BS4App\gulpfile.js
  [13:35:36] Starting 'compile-sass'...
  [13:35:36] Finished 'compile-sass' after 8.47 ms

  Watching build tasks has finished.|
```

After the `compile-sass` task has completed, you should see a `bootstrap.css` file inside the `wwwroot\css` folder. Your project layout should be similar to the following inside the Visual Studio Code Explorer:

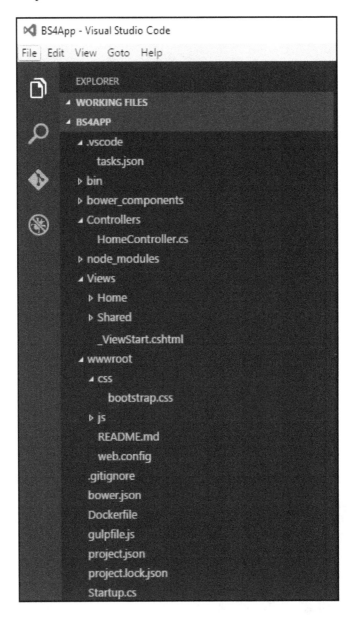

Creating a MVC layout page

The last step in creating a Bootstrap 4 enabled ASP.NET MVC project is to create a master layout page that will reference the Bootstrap CSS and JavaScript files. To create the layout page, complete the following steps:

1. Add a new file called _Layout.cshtml to the Views\Shared folder.
2. Add the following HTML to the file:

```
<!DOCTYPE html>
<html>
<head>
    <meta charset="utf-8" />
    <meta name="viewport" content="width=device-width,
     initial-scale=1.0" />
    <title>My Bootstrap Site</title>
    <link rel="stylesheet" href="~/css/bootstrap.css" />
</head>
<body>

    <div class="container body-content">
        @RenderBody()
        <hr />
        <footer>
            <p>&copy; @DateTime.Now.Year - Your Bootstrap 4
site</p>
        </footer>
    </div>

</body>
</html>
```

3. Save the file.
4. In order to use the layout file, add a new file called Index.cshtml to the Views/Home folder and set its contents to the following:

```
@{
    Layout="~/Views/Shared/_Layout.cshtml";
}
<h1>This is my Bootstrap 4 site. </h1>
```

Testing the site

In order to test the site, you'll need to switch back to the command prompt and enter the following command in order to start the Kestrel web server and run your site:

```
dotnet run
```

A message will be displayed, stating that the web server is listening on `http://localhost:5000`. Open your browser and navigate to the URL. You should see your website running inside the browser with the default Bootstrap 4 styling.

Summary

In this chapter, you were introduced to the new editor; Visual Studio Code from Microsoft, and saw how you can use it to create an ASP.NET MVC site that uses Bootstrap 4 on Windows, Linux, and OS X.

This is also the last chapter of this book and by now you should be fairly comfortable with using Bootstrap in your own ASP.NET MVC projects. You should also be a bit more familiar with the new ASP.NET Core and the new package managers and task runners it uses.

Make sure you download the sample project that accompanies this book from the Packt website or from the Github repository at `https://github.com/Pietervdw/bootstrap-for-aspnetmvc` in order to see the examples mentioned in action.

Thank you for reading. Until next time, keep coding!

Bootstrap Resources

The Bootstrap community is a vibrant and vast one. Following, in no particular order, is a list of Bootstrap resources available on the Internet.

Themes

Following are the free and premium HTML themes based on Bootstrap:

URL	Description
http://startbootstrap.com/	Free HTML starter templates and themes for Bootstrap.
https://wrapbootstrap.com/	A marketplace for premium themes and templates for Bootstrap.
http://bit.ly/ThemeForestHtml	Themeforest has over 5000 premium HTML templates, many based on Bootstrap, some not.
http://www.prepbootstrap.com/	Free Bootstrap themes, templates, and other widgets with complete code examples.
http://bootstrapzero.com/	Open source Bootstrap themes and templates.
http://bootswatch.com/	Free themes for Bootstrap
http://setbootstrap.com/	Free Bootstrap themes and templates

Add-ons

Additional add-ons, plugins, and components for Bootstrap are as follows:

URL	Description
`http://getfuelux.com/`	FuelUX provides additional controls and enhancements for Bootstrap-like date pickers, spinners, trees, and form wizards.
`http://bit.ly/JasnyBoot strap`	Jasny Bootstrap provides some enhancements to exciting components like label buttons and anchored alerts.
`http://bit.ly/Bootstrap Notify`	Bootstrap notify makes it easier to display alert style notifications to your users.
`http://bootstrapformhel pers.com/`	Bootstrap form helpers are a plugin to help enhance your forms. Includes color pickers, sliders, and so on.
`http://www.bootstrap-sw itch.org/`	Turn your check boxes into iOS-style switch controls.
`http://bit.ly/BSAppWiz`	Add multi-step, wizard-like interfaces to your forms with the Bootstrap Application Wizard
`http://bit.ly/TypeAhead`	A plugin by Twitter. Add autocomplete to your forms.
`http://bit.ly/1NjDwpD`	X-editable—Create editable elements on your page.
`http://bootboxjs.com/`	Flexible dialogs
`http://bit.ly/1QRU2Yy`	Bootstrap file upload
`http://bit.ly/1NUFehr`	Bootstrap password strength indicator
`http://bit.ly/1THpCf`	Bootstrap Mega menu
`http://bit.ly/1SLum5v`	Image gallery for Bootstrap
`http://bit.ly/1Y7h7MK`	Ladda buttons—buttons with built-in loading indicators.
`http://www.plupload.com`	Multi-runtime file uploader
`http://ckeditor.com`	WYSIWYG text editor
`http://bit.ly/1OdE4rW`	Ion.RangeSlider —a responsive range slider
`http://bit.ly/1WHvuIZ`	Context-menu

Editors and generators

Tools that help you design and build your Bootstrap site are as follows:

URL	Description
`http://www.bootstrapbundle.com/`	ASP.Net MVC Bootstrap project and item templates for Visual Studio 2015
`http://www.layoutit.com/`	Drag-and-drop interface builder for Bootstrap
`https://jetstrap.com/`	Visual interface building tool for Bootstrap
`http://www.bootply.com/`	Visual editor for rapidly building interfaces for Bootstrap.
`http://bit.ly/BSMagic`	Bootstrap Magic. Easily create your own theme for Bootstrap.
`http://paintstrap.com/`	Generate Bootstrap themes using a COLOURLovers color scheme.
`http://www.bootstrapdesigner.com/`	Generate websites or templates for Bootstrap.
`http://bit.ly/1X7NGf6`	Blocks v.3 Drag-and-drop builder for Bootstrap
`http://shoelace.io/`	Visual Bootstrap grid builder

Index

A

accordion/collapse component
  about 92
  using 94
add-ons, Bootstrap
  references 168
Alert Tag Helper
  using 112
alerts 72, 73
Amazon CloudFront
  reference 27
animated progress bar 75
ASP.NET MVC project
  creating 116
  DataTables, adding to 134
Atom Shell 152
Atom
  reference 152

B

badges
  about 60
  creating 61
basic forms 46, 47
basic navbar 54
basic progress bar 74
Bootstrap 4 Admin Dashboard
  reference link 115
Bootstrap 4 Alpha installation sources
  reference 9
Bootstrap 4 files
  adding, Bower used 15, 160, 161
Bootstrap 4
  reference 7
Bootstrap Alert Tag Helper
  creating 111

Bootstrap button Tag Helper
  creating 109, 110
  using 110
Bootstrap buttons
  about 44, 45
  outline buttons 45
Bootstrap community 167
Bootstrap components
  badges 60
  breadcrumbs 63
  list groups 58
  media object 61
  navigation bar 53
Bootstrap distributions
  files 7
Bootstrap fonts/icons 8
Bootstrap Grid components
  about 30
  columns 31, 32
  containers 30
  rows 30
Bootstrap grid system 30
Bootstrap HTML elements
  about 32
  buttons 44, 45
  tables 33
Bootstrap JavaScript files 8
Bootstrap library
  referencing, from CDN 26
Bootstrap resources
  references 167, 168, 169
Bootstrap Sass files
  compiling, Gulp used 18, 162, 164
Bootstrap source files 8
Bootstrap style sheets 8
Bootstrap styling
  adding, to jQuery DataTables plugin 135, 136

Bootstrap tables
  about 33
  Contextual table classes 41, 42, 43
  MVC List View page, scaffolding 34
  MVC Scaffolding, enabling 33, 35, 36, 37
  reference 41
  responsive tables 43
  smaller tables 43
  styling 38, 40, 41
Bootstrap themes 114
Bootstrap Zero
  reference link 114
Bower
  reference 15
  used, for adding Bootstrap 4 files 15, 160, 161
breadcrumbs 63
built-in HTML Helpers 100
built-in Tag Helpers 100
button dropdowns 71

C

cards 75, 76, 77
carousel component 94, 95, 96
Chart.js
  reference link 126
charts
  adding, to view 126
cloudscribe.Web.Pagination library 68
columns 31, 32
containers 30
Content Delivery Network (CDN)
  about 134
  Bootstrap library, referencing from 26
contextual progress bars 74
CSS pre-processors 9

D

data attributes
  versus programmatic API 79, 80
data
  displaying, in jQuery DataTables plugin 136,
    137, 140, 141
  loading, in jQuery DataTables 136, 137, 140,
    141
DataTables CDN

references 134, 136
different page views
  adding 123
dropdowns
  cascading 80

E

editors and generators, Bootstrap
  references 169
Electron framework 152
empty ASP.NET MVC site
  Bootstrap, adding manually 10
  creating 9
  default route controller and view, creating 12, 13,
    14
  MVC and static files, enabling 11
empty ASP.NET project
  ASP.NET MVC, enabling 156, 157
  creating 154
  default route controller, adding 158, 159
  scaffolding, Yeoman used 154, 155
  static files, enabling 156, 157
  view, adding 158, 159
extension methods
  extension method helper, using in view 106
  reference link 105
  used, for creating helpers 105
extensions, jQuery DataTables plugin
  about 143
  ColReorder 144, 145
  ColVis 146, 147
  copy and print button extension 147, 148, 149

F

figures 51, 52
files, in Bootstrap distribution
  about 7
  fonts/icons 8
  JavaScript files 8
  source files 8
  style sheets 8
Flot
  reference link 126
Font Awesome
  about 23

installing 24
reference 8, 23
forms
about 46
basic forms 46, 47
grid-based forms 48
inline forms 47
vertical forms 46, 47

G

GitHub's Octicons
reference 8
Google Charts
adding, to view 127, 128
adding, to views 126
reference link 126
used, for server-side data processing 128, 129
Google Hosted Libraries
reference 27
grid-based forms 48
Gulp npm packages
adding 18
Gulp tasks
binding, to Visual Studio events 22, 23
running 21, 22
Gulp-Sass compilation
enabling 20
Gulp
about 20
reference 20
used, for compiling Bootstrap Sass files 18, 162, 164

H

helpers
creating, with extension methods 105
home controller
view, adding for 121, 122
HTML Helpers
about 99
creating, with static methods 102, 104
reference link 100

I

images 49
inline forms 47
input groups 69
IntelliSense 152
issues, for Bootstrap 4 on GitHub
reference 56

J

jQuery DataTables plugin
about 133, 134, 141
adding, to ASP.NET MVC project 134
Bootstrap styling, adding to 135, 136
CDN, using 135
data, displaying in 136, 137, 140, 141
data, loading in 136, 137, 140, 141
DataTables Bower package, using 134, 135
date sorting, enabling 142
extensions 143
reference 141
rendering 143

L

list groups 58, 59

M

master layout
creating 119
MaxCDN
reference 27
media object 61
modal dialogs
animation 86
sizes 86
using 84
Moment.js
about 142
reference 142
Moris.js
reference link 126
MVC layout page
creating 25, 165
MVC Tag Helpers
reference link 110

N

navbar color schemes 57, 58
navigation bar
  about 53
  basic navbar 54
  responsive navbar 54, 56
  with dropdown menus 56, 57
NPM
  installing, steps 154
NuGet 16

O

outline buttons 45

P

paged list
  creating 65
pagination 64
popovers 90
prebuilt HTML templates
  working with 113, 114
progress bars
  about 73
  animated progress bar 75
  basic progress bars 74
  contextual progress bars 74
  striped progress bar 75

R

responsive navbar 54, 56
rows 30

S

Sass
  reference 18
self-closing helpers
  creating 106, 107, 108
  using, in view 108, 109

static method helper
  using, in view 104
static methods
  static method helper, using in view 104
  used, for creating HTML Helpers 102
striped progress bar 75

T

table body element 37
table head element 37
tabs 87, 88
Tag Helpers
  about 99
  and HTML Helpers, differentiating 101, 102
  reference link 101
Themeforest
  reference link 114
themes, Bootstrap
  references 167
tooltips 89

V

vertical forms 46, 47
view
  adding, for home controller 121, 122
  charts, adding to 126
  Google Charts, adding 126, 127, 128
Visual Studio Code
  about 151, 152
  installing 152
  reference 152
  reference, for setup 154
Visual Studio events
  Gulp tasks, binding to 22, 23

Y

Yeoman
  used, for scaffolding empty ASP.NET project 154, 155